SOUTH WEST
HERITAGE STEAM RAILWAYS

A HISTORY AND GUIDE

Adrian Harris

HALSGROVE

Previous page: *The meandering line heads south following the River Dart until we reach Kingswear. Seen here heading back north towards Paignton is* **Lydham Manor No.7827**. *5 March 2013.*

GWR 4575 Class 2-6-2T **No.5552** *works hard on the long climb past Westheath towards Bodmin General Station. 31 December 2011.*

First published in Great Britain in 2014

British Library Cataloguing-in-Publication Data
A CIP record for this title is available from the British Library

ISBN 978 0 85704 229 3

HALSGROVE
Halsgrove House,
Ryelands Business Park,
Bagley Road, Wellington, Somerset TA21 9PZ
Tel: 01823 653777 Fax: 01823 216796
email: sales@halsgrove.com
website: www.halsgrove.com

Printed and bound in China by Everbest Printing Co Ltd

CONTENTS

No.43106, an LMS 2-6-0 Ivatt Class 4 locomotive, arrives at Williton heading north towards Minehead with a train from Stogumber. 5 October 2012.

DEDICATIONS

I would like to say a big thank you to the following people who have helped me throughout this project…

My wife Gillian, a wonderful companion who has been so supportive and very patient. Christine for all the encouragement and keeping me focused. Francis for his general support and technical guidance. Colin, for supplying the final few photos after I had misplaced mine and felt like giving up! And last but not least, my mother Audrey Harris, who tirelessly took me to watch the steam trains at Exeter Central Station so regularly 'because I always seemed to enjoy them so much' and without whom I may never have developed my love for steam.

*A landscape so typical from the early twentieth century. Due to the wonderful heritage steam railways which now flourish in the UK, nostalgic scenes like this can still be enjoyed today. Ex-GWR designed Manor Class 4-6-0 **No.7828 Odney Manor** passes Leigh Cattle Creep on the West Somerset Railway. 6 October 2013.*

FOREWORD

For the purpose of this book heritage railways are considered to be those that run historic locomotives and rolling stock. Other than this title grouping there are many differences in the ways in which the various rail companies covered in this book operate. Most are run mainly by volunteers (perhaps a perfect example of Cameron's Big Society in action!), some have a few paid full time staff – usually in the managerial or engineering departments, while another runs as a totally commercial concern throughout.

Most heritage railways try to preserve the past and have restored, or more usually are in the continuous process of restoring, every facet and detail of their operation, with the intention of portraying an accurate representation of a particular period in time – generally ranging from the post Second World War years, to just before the demise of steam in the late 1960s. However this doesn't tell the whole story, because some engines built as much as 70 years earlier were still in everyday use right up until that end came. Various companies, museums, associations and individuals, have managed to acquire, restore and in certain cases build replicas of, steam engines and rolling stock from a far earlier age. Some of them date back to the very beginning of the railway revolution and these are also frequently found either on display, or in use on heritage lines throughout the country. Conversely, many rail preservation societies spurred on by a different generation of enthusiasts, now have collections of historic diesel locomotives from latter days and although most commonly seen in a supporting role, they are more frequently starring in their own special gala events.

The key thing that all the railways mentioned in this book do have in common, is that in one way or another, they provide a taste of the historic steam age experience from a golden age of rail travel.

A very special mention has to go to all the volunteers and donors who have seen these major projects through to the wonderful operations which we see running today and without whom virtually all of the UKs heritage railways would not be able to run.

As I researched the material for this project, reading the tales of determination and tenacity of the many people who fought so desperately hard to rebuild our heritage lines, it made me feel very humble indeed and so privileged that I am now able to ride on 'their' magnificent railways. I take my hat off to you all.

ABOUT THIS BOOK

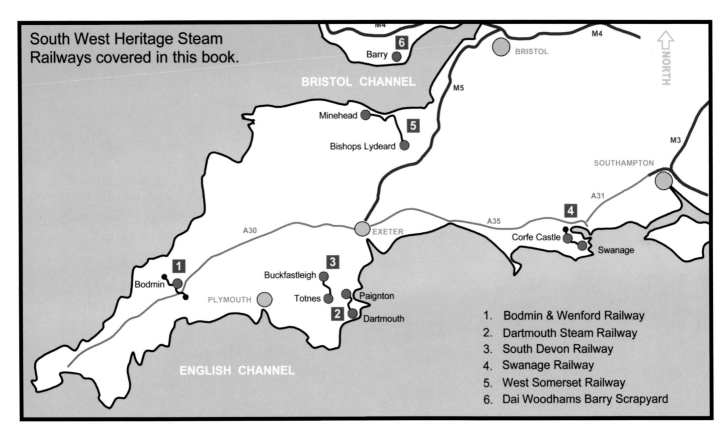

South West Heritage Steam Railways covered in this book.

1. Bodmin & Wenford Railway
2. Dartmouth Steam Railway
3. South Devon Railway
4. Swanage Railway
5. West Somerset Railway
6. Dai Woodhams Barry Scrapyard

Track Layout and Station Locations

A map is provided in the relevant chapter for each heritage railway showing the track layout, stations and halts, plus feeder roads, nearby towns and other prominent landmarks.

Heritage Railway Locomotive Stock Listed in this Book

Although heritage railways generally own many of their regular usage engines, lots of preserved locomotives in the UK are actually owned by groups of private individuals and are on long term loan or hire to specific railways. Locomotives also frequently move between heritage railways and although sometimes this is only for a brief period, such as for a particular gala, it is not uncommon for a locomotive to be at another railway for a whole season, or even for many years. As this situation is in a constant state of flux, it would be all but impossible to write definitive lists of locomotives and rolling stock for each line. Therefore those presented later in this book, are only intended as a guide to stock currently normally associated with each railway circa 2012-2013.

The Photographic Journey

Other than those arranged in the introduction, the photographs in this book are presented in their respective chapters, by way of a journey along each railway travelling from one end to the other. In this way, the reader is able to put the route into context and in essence experience a sense of place, as if following the footsteps of a journeyman travelling along each of the heritage lines.

Terminology

The author has tried to keep railway specific non-general terminology to a minimum. However, because a few terms expressed may be unknown to those with little previous knowledge of railways and also some having fallen out of common usage since the demise of steam locomotives, you will find a glossary of these terms along with explanations in the Appendix.

Photograph Acknowledgements

All the photographs in this book were taken by the author Adrian Harris, with the exception of the Barry Scrapyard images which were kindly supplied by Colin Yelland (due to the author having misplaced his in the intervening 48 years!).

Copyright

With the exception of the Barry Scrapyard images which are the copyright of Colin Yelland, all graphics, photographs and text in this publication were produced by and are copyright of the author Adrian Harris. No content from this publication may be reproduced in print, or transmitted electronically or in digital form, or be used on any social website, or other types of website or blog of any sort, without previously obtained written permission. The author asserts his moral rights.

INTRODUCTION

How Heritage Railways in the UK Came to Be

Heritage Railways come in many forms, shapes, sizes and gauges, but this book is primarily looking at 'standard gauge' heritage lines where the rails are four feet eight and a half inches apart (4ft 8½" or 1,435mm). This gauge was first established at Willington Colliery near Newcastle-upon-Tyne in 1764 and with few exceptions – India, Southern Africa, Ireland, Spain, Japan and Russia – has also been accepted as the world standard.

In Great Britain the government played little part in the development of the railways but left it to hundreds of entrepreneurial private companies. Over the decades, many of the smaller lines were gradually swallowed up by the larger corporations who permanently fought each other bitterly for greater control, but even they eventually acknowledged the advantages of working together and slowly began to enter into closer working arrangements.

Sadly none of the 82000 class tank locomotives made it into preservation and this particular one was only ten years old when finally broken for scrap in 1965 at Birds in Long Marston. Photographed by the author in 1964, BR Standard Class 3MT 2-6-2 tank engine **No.82039** *arrives at Exeter Central Station during its last year operating from the depot at Exmouth Junction.*

Fortunately not all locomotives went to Birds for breaking and although this particular West Country Class Bulleid pacific **No.34014 Budleigh Salterton** *photographed while being serviced at the Exmouth Junction depot in 1964 didn't survive, a very good example No.34028 Eddystone was saved and is currently in regular service on the Swanage heritage railway.*

Understandably, there was a high degree of government control throughout the First World War (a period which exhausted the railways) and, in 1923, around 150 of the main railway companies were grouped into the 'Big 4'. These were the GWR – Great Western Railway, the LMS – London Midland & Scottish, the LNER – London & North Eastern Railway and the SR – Southern Railway. After the Second World War Britain's rail system was further depleted and in need of much reinvestment. It was against this background that in 1948 the Big 4 were amalgamated and nationalised to become BR – British Railways.

In 1955 a rapid modernisation plan was proposed, which along with the Beeching Report of 1963, saw the advent of diesel and electric power. And so, the ancient and dirty pre-Victorian steam power source for locomotives was replaced and along with it, thousands of miles of track and a massive part of Britain's industrial heritage, that had over the previous century grown to be a seamless part of the United Kingdom's landscape.

For well over a century Britain had exported railways and steam engines to the whole world and as the 1960s dawned, a growing few began to realise that within a decade much of this history would be gone forever.

The Beginnings of Historical Railway Preservation

The Science Museum in London (originally known as the Patent Office Museum) had actually started collecting railway artefacts as far back as 1862 when it acquired Stephenson's Rocket – the winner at the Rainhill Trials and historical fore-runner of all subsequent steam locomotives. From the late 1800s, railway companies had also begun preserving their past and, in 1927, the LNER opened a museum in York dedicated to railways. Through the efforts of the Stephenson Locomotive Society, that same year also saw the first locomotive to be privately preserved, an ex-London, Brighton and South Coast Railway 0-4-2 'Gladstone'.

Just before the Second World War, the 'Big 4' had all started their own collections and these were finally brought together in 1948 during their nationalisation. A 'curator of historical relics' was finally appointed for the nationalised industry in 1951 and a collecting policy was implemented to tell the story of the Britain's railways.

British Rail in liaison with the Science Museum, developed a National Railway Museum to house this massive and ever expanding collection at Leeman Road in York, at a former steam locomotive depot in 1975. This collection of locomotives spanning fifteen decades of steam currently stands at around 87 and many of these, although destined initially only for static preservation, have now been restored to working order and can be seen in use at various heritage railways around the UK.

The Relevance of Dai Woodham's Barry Scrapyard

A consequence of the 1955 Modernisation Plan and 1963 Beeching Report meant the scrapping of 16,000 steam locomotives, halving of the 1.25 million wagon stock and the removal of thousands of miles of rails.

When the author visited Dai Woodham's Barry Scrapyard in 1965, many hundreds of locomotives were parked up nose to tail on line after line of track. 'It was a shocking and emotional sight to see these once proud giants of steam which had hissed and roared and breathed life with every move of their existence, to now be laying there so still and deathly quiet'. The never to be forgotten impression, was that of a mass grave.

Twenty years after the author visited Dai Woodham's Barry Scrapyard, these photos were taken by Colin Yelland when he visited the yard with his family in November 1985. By then many of the engines had already been removed by preservation groups and although most of those remaining had also been earmarked, alas many were in a horrendous state.

Pilfering for spare parts was starting to be a major concern, hence the boldly painted notices staking claims and encouraging groups to leave each other's purchases well alone.

Studying the condition of the locomotives shown in the photo to the left and the two photos overleaf, gives some idea of the enormity of the restoration task that was faced. In the early days of preservation it must have taken huge leaps of faith to believe that these wonderful giants of our industrial age could ever steam again.

Although many new steam engines were still to be built, large scale disposal started in 1959. As the major BR works could not cope with the huge amount of condemned locomotives and stock which were arriving for cutting up, the disposal had to be put out to private companies and the Woodham Brothers of Barry in Wales became one of the major contractors. At first Woodham's only bought a small amount to scrap, but soon the quantity of wagons and locomotives increased to the extent that extra sidings had to be acquired to store the condemned stock.

Unlike many of the other scrapyards who were also busy cutting up ex-BR stock, Dai Woodham decided that as wagons were by far the easiest to scrap, the lines of rapidly multiplying locomotives could be saved for a later 'rainy day'. As a result, by August 1968 there were still 217 locomotives remaining at the Barry scrapyard.

Health and safety rules being far less rigorous than they are now, meant that steam enthusiasts from throughout the UK could visit the row upon row of ghostly locomotives awaiting their fate at Barry Island, a location which soon became a regular pilgrimage site for the emerging steam railway preservation movement.

Dai Woodham's Barry Scrapyard in November 1985. Photographs courtesy of Colin Yelland.

Enthusiasts to the Fore

As the Beeching axe began to fall on loss-making lines up and down the country, small groups of railway enthusiasts began to think the unthinkable. If British Railways took away the trains, could hard-working amateurs bring them back – if not for outright profit perhaps, then for pleasure? Proof that this idea could work came from Wales, where the narrow-gauge Tal-y-llyn Railway had already been running since 1951 as the first preserved railway in the world and staffed almost entirely by volunteers.

During the mid to late '60s it was almost as if the railway revolution was regenerating, small groups of like minded individuals were gathering together all over the UK, to try and preserve much of what the National Collection had failed to do.

Many classes of locomotives had already become extinct and other than those in the National Collection, plus a small number of privately bought locos, the lines of engines decaying at Barry were now the only source of steam locomotives left to preserve for the future. But even as scrap, due to their extensive use of high-grade steel forgings and plate, lots of cast iron, plus brass, copper and bronze for their boiler fittings, steam locomotives are still very valuable items, hence would-be preservationists had no other option but to start fund-raising campaigns.

Last Chance Saloon

The Barry Steam Locomotive Action Group was formed in 1979 to attempt to put together potential purchasers, funders and the Woodham Brothers. This was an important last ditch move, as by then nearly all the railway wagons had been scrapped and work would shortly be starting on cutting up the last ever remaining steam locomotives. Although three more were in fact lost during the summer of 1980 when the Barry yard went through a very quiet work period, fortunately the action group largely succeeded in their quest and saved many more.

It soon became standard practice for Woodham's to allow preservation groups to pay a deposit for a particular locomotive which was then reserved until the group could pay for the locomotive in full and then arrange transport. At first preservationists started buying 'the better examples' which tended to be the later engines, as these were the easiest to return to working order. And so, the railway preservation boom began.

Saving the Branch Lines

In England, the standard-gauge pioneers included the Bluebell Railway in Sussex, the Dart Valley Railway in Devon, and the Keighley and Worth Valley Railway in Yorkshire. Though their activities were frowned upon in official circles, these railways successfully managed to start running passenger trains by taking advantage of the Light Railway Order legislation, a provision dating from the 1900s, exempting them from having to have the same costly safety and signalling systems in place as British Railways – but only so long as their trains were run at speeds of no faster than 25 miles per hour!

Buying a locomotive is one thing, but restoring it to working order, having somewhere to put it, and a line to run upon afterwards, is quite another. So when British Rail decided to ban all steam locomotives – except the ex-LNER pacific 'Flying Scotsman' owned by businessman Alan Pegler – from running over its tracks in 1968, the immediate future for preserved steam looked as though it would lie on solely the private lines. Thus some of the more far-sighted railways began to equip themselves with the heavy machinery needed to undertake the more major overhauls that steam requires, as realisation was dawning that working locomotives – unlike museum exhibits – still wore out, even under the light duties expected of them working three or four coach trains on a 5 to 15 mile branch line.

The Railway Heritage Committee (RHC)

The RHC is a national body set up by central government with the function of designating which records and artefacts are historically significant and therefore should be permanently preserved. Their Mission Statement highlights that *'the Railway Heritage Committee is established by statute to secure the preservation of evidence which is significant to the railways' history.'* However in early 2013, the government announced that the RHC would be disbanded by the end of March 2013 and its powers transferred to the Science Museum.

Heritage Railway Association (HRA)

The HRA is a body which has over 250 corporate members and represents the interests of the majority of heritage and tourist railways, tramways, railway preservation groups and most of the railway museums and steam centres within both the UK, and Ireland. The major part of their mission is to represent members' interests to Government and other bodies, and also to ensure high standards are met by requiring its members to conform to the HRA Code of Practice.

The Future

Heritage railways have generally had a boom time since the new millennium and despite the economic downturn since 2008, tourists and enthusiast have still flocked to experience the 'steam dream'. However shortly after the start of the second decade, long spells of bad weather have had a very adverse affect. Not only has the incessant rain, dark grey skies and miserable cold kept the public away, it has also caused a few of the major lines to suffer severe infrastructure failures, which in some cases has caused the closure of those lines for large periods of time when they could least afford it.

Heartbreakingly, metal theft has also been a serious issue of late, not only for all UK heritage, but also for British mainline rail. For mainline rail metal theft has severe safety implications, but the restricted speeds enforced on heritage lines means that the safety issue is less of a factor. However, the loss of parts on heritage lines truly is disastrous as all the locos are historic artefacts, many with unique fitments and no patterns are available to manufacture replacements when those parts are stolen.

Even so, as I write this the future of UK heritage railways in general looks readily assured. As not only are the current heritage lines being further developed (with some even expanding their track beds along former routes), but amazingly more historic lines are actually still being rescued from obscurity and being opened for the public.

It is heart-warming to see so many young people volunteering and getting involved in all aspects of running the railways and as long as this continues, heritage rail promises to have a very long future indeed.

BODMIN & WENFORD RAILWAY

History of the Bodmin & Wenford Railway

The Bodmin & Wenford Railway is based at Bodmin in Cornwall. It is currently operated by the Bodmin & Wenford Railway PLC in association with the Bodmin & Wenford Railway Trust and the Bodmin Railway Preservation Society. A number of other smaller organisations also support the running of the railway which operates under the *Bodmin Railway Centre Light Railway Order 1989*.

The original line was commissioned by Sir William Molesworth in 1832 to run from Bodmin to Wadebridge. The branch line from Bodmin Road (Parkway) to Bodmin was opened in 1887 and further extended to Boscarne Junction to join up with the existing Bodmin & Wadebridge Railway in 1888.

When British Railways finally closed the line in 1983 a group of enthusiasts intent on preserving Bodmin's railway got together and formed the Bodmin Railway Preservation Society (June 1984) with the aim of re-opening the Railway and running preserved steam engines. Bodmin & Wenford Railway PLC was registered in February 1985 to raise capital and run the business side.

Although North Cornwall District Council (NCDC) bought the land, the B&W had to buy the track and at that time the whole line was simply not affordable. It was eventually decided to purchase the track from Bodmin Parkway through to Bodmin General and on to Boscarne Junction – an investment that was a huge risk.

The purchase from BR was completed by the council in March 1986 which allowed track work to start and also provided room for rolling stock. However, complete occupancy didn't start until more than three years later (1989) as the station buildings were let to a furniture company and NCDC needed to terminate the lease.

Shortly after the *Cornish Steam Locomotive Preservation Society* (CSLPS) was formed in 1974 an open day was held at Par. The CSLPS mainly aimed to preserve industrial locos and in 1977 moved to Bugle and started the Bugle Steam Railway. In 1986, with a number of locomotives and wagons in its care, the society moved its base to Bodmin General Station, thus providing locomotives for the then infant Bodmin & Wenford Railway.

We will start our pictorial journey along the Bodmin and Wenford Railway at its southernmost terminus, Bodmin Parkway. It shares the station with the main-line and where there is also a through rail connection for special excursions.

*Home based ex-GWR 4575 Class 2-6-2 Prairie Tank **No.5552** heads away from Parkway, bearing northwest towards Bodmin General. 8 April 2011.*

The CSLPS biggest recent project was the complete restoration of *Alfred* and *Judy* the 0-4-0 saddle tank Pit to Port twins which are now resident at the B&W. The twins also make frequent and popular guest appearances at various other heritage lines around the country.

On 1 June 1986 B&W held their first Open Day to the public. Fortunately the weather was dry and pickup goods routines were performed at intervals throughout the day which was a great success. Subsequently, in 1987, the *Bodmin & Wenford Railway Trust* was formed to promote education about the railway's heritage and to encourage public support.

1988 saw the introduction of steam-hauled brake van rides but it was not until 1989 that a Light Railway Order (LRO) was granted which allowed an extension of operations. By way of celebration, passenger services were extended 1 mile from Bodmin General on the very next day! An ex-HM Devonport Dockyard Bagnal 0-4-0 saddle tank *No19* worked those first Bodmin & Wenford trains.

In June 1990 the Bodmin & Wenford Railway commenced a scheduled daily timetable running south-east from Bodmin General to Bodmin Parkway. Colesloggett Halt was built between these two termini and opened in 1992. The final part of the line which runs north-west from Bodmin General to Boscarne Junction was re-opened in 1996. Scheduled running days are now typically well over 200 per annum.

Besides the scheduled timetable, the B&W also runs a series of special Steam Gala events throughout the year plus Santa Specials, Postman Pat days, Murder Mystery Specials, Footplate Experience Courses and Pasty/Bistro Specials. A luxury Dining Train is also available for private hire.

Website links:
- Further information on the Bodmin and Wenford Railway can be obtained from their website – *www.bodminrailway.co.uk*
- Further information about the Bodmin Railway Preservation Society can be obtained from their website – *www.bodminrailwaypreservationsociety.co.uk*

Immediately after leaving Bodmin Parkway the line veers right and crosses Bodmin Road Viaduct by Dreasonmoor Wood. Seen here hauling a short mixed traffic during the Bodmin and Wenford Spring Steam Spectacular Gala is another home-based locomotive, an ex-LSWR Beattie Well Tank Class 2-4-0WT **No.30587**. *20 April 2012.*

Track Layout and Stations

The Bodmin & Wenford Railway is 6½ miles in length and the track layout is slightly unusual in that it forms a 'Y'. Thus it has three termini along a single line, with Bodmin General – the principal station, in the middle (effectively at the base of the 'Y').

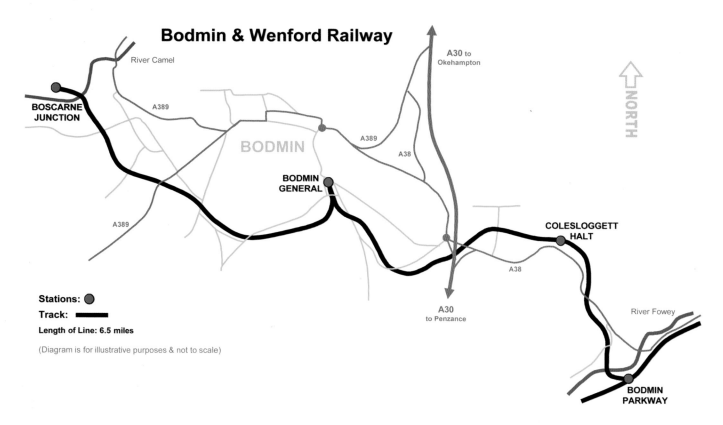

Bodmin General is the highest station on the line and engines can be heard working very hard when heading towards it from either direction. It is for this reason that all engines face towards it and make a spectacular sight when steaming chimney first through the cuttings, valleys and woods.

Starting our journey from Bodmin Parkway, the line turns northward across Bodmin Road Viaduct into woodland where the engines start their long and hard homeward bound climb. Passing under Dreason Bridge the line breaks out into the open turning west at Charlie's Gate, before briefly tunnelling under the main A38 while still climbing on through Newpark Wood towards Colesloggett Halt. From here the line stays in a cutting heading once more under the A38 and starts to level out into the open just before approaching Quarry Curve and the Walker Lines Industrial Estate on the edge of Bodmin town. Then a gentle run-in through the outskirts of Bodmin leads the train into the town centre terminus at Bodmin General Station.

From the Boscarne Junction direction, the line first heads east, then turns southward over the River Camel before bearing east once more along mixed farmland and cuttings. Here engines labour intensively up the long steep cutting that runs under the A389 road bridge before making their way out into the open at Westheath. Still rising, the line continues its tree-clad climb all the way back to Checkrail Curve just before entering the railway's main terminus at Bodmin General.

Bodmin General: The station has been beautifully restored to reflect the 1950s and has a period buffet serving a good variety of hot and cold food and drinks. It also has a wheelchair accessible toilet and baby change facilities. A well-stocked gift and souvenir shop also sells railway books, videos, various model railway items and children's toys. There are two locomotive sheds at Bodmin General and visitors are welcome to see the restoration and repair work being carried out on Roads 1 and 2. There is a small free car park plus plenty of nearby on-road parking.

Bodmin Parkway: Travelling south-east the line terminates at Bodmin Parkway (originally called Bodmin Road), a main-line station where B&W shares the platform 3 island with London-bound trains from Penzance. The Bodmin & Wenford Railway operate a café at this station which was converted from the old Signal Box and now offer hot drinks and sandwiches to all travellers. The station has toilets and a large adjacent council maintained car park.

Boscarne Junction: This is now the north-west terminus of the B&W Railway, although originally Boscarne Junction was the junction where the Bodmin & Wadebridge Railway met the Great Western Railway. The station has a traditional stone-built waiting room with paintwork in Southern green and a 'run-around' loop for the engine. There are many routes for walkers and cyclists but no adjacent car access for the public to this station.

Colesloggett Halt: A new station built in 1993 to serve an adjacent Farm Park which has now closed. This small halt with its open wooden shelter is built on a steep gradient; hence trains only stop when heading downhill from Bodmin General to Bodmin Parkway. There are two access routes to this halt both of which are a five minute walk.

*Already working hard on the start of the long climb back to Bodmin General, Isle of Wight-based visitor **Calbourne**, an Adams-built ex-LSWR O2 Class 0-4-4 Tank **No.24**, pilots a Bodmin-based Drummond T9 4-4-0 Greyhound **No.30120**, as they approach Dreason Bridge. 20 April 2012.*

A GWR Class 2-8-0 Tank **No.4247** *painted in BR black, passes under Dreason Bridge climbing its way towards Charlie's Gate. 11 March 2012.*

Bodmin & Wenford Railway typical 'standard' daily timetable

Shown below is an example B&W daily timetable. Although the times are typical, they should not be taken literally as times may be adjusted from season to season as needs change. However it does give an idea of the frequency of trains and travel times between stations on a normal service day.

RED TIMETABLE	(All steam)	a.m.	a.m.	p.m.	p.m.	p.m.
BODMIN GENERAL	Depart	**10.30**	**11.45**	**1.00**	**2.15**	**3.30**
COLESLOGGETT HALT	Depart	10.40	---	1.10	---	3.40
BODMIN PARKWAY	Arrive	10.47	---	1.17	---	3.47
BOSCARNE JCN	Arrive	---	12.00	--	2.30	--
		a.m.	p.m.	p.m.	p.m.	p.m.
BOSCARNE JCN	Depart	---	12.10	--	2.40	--
BODMIN PARKWAY	Depart	11.00	---	1.30	--	4.00
BODMIN GENERAL	Arrive	**11.20**	**11.27**	**1.50**	**2.57**	**4.20**

NOTE: Trains call at Colesloggett Halt **ONLY** on the outward journey from Bodmin General to Bodmin Parkway

During peak season and on special galas, a two train running system is frequently in operation on the B&W which almost doubles the amount of trains running daily. However, on quiet days and especially towards winter, the timetable may typically be reduced to four trains per day. There are also frequent evening and late night specials for various events with running times posted separately on the B&W website.

LOCOMOTIVES ON THE BODMIN & WENFORD RAILWAY   **Circa 2012/2013**

The list below is only intended as a guide to stock recently associated with the line.

STEAM LOCOMOTIVES

Number/Description		Condition/Info
5552	GWR 4575 Class 2-6-2T	Serviceable
4247	GWR 42xx Class 2-8-0T	Serviceable
6435	GWR 64xx Class 0-6-0PT	Undergoing Overhaul
2962	Bagnall 0-4-0ST *No.19*	Serviceable
3058	Bagnall 0-4-0ST *Alfred*	Serviceable
2572	Bagnall 0-4-0ST *Judy*	Serviceable
3121	Bagnall 0-4-0 Fireless	Stored
30587	LSWR Beattie 2-4-0WT	Serviceable
30120	LSWR T9 4-4-0	Serviceable

DIESEL LOCOMOTIVES

Number/Description	Condition/Info	
50042 / D442	BR Class 50 Co-Co Diesel	Serviceable
47306 / D1787	BR Class 47 Co-Co Diesel	Serviceable
37142 / D6842	BR Class 37 Co-Co Diesel	Undergoing Overhaul
33110 / D6527	BR Class 33 Bo-Bo Diesel	Serviceable
08444 / D3559	BR Class 08 Diesel	Serviceable
D3452	BR Class 10 Diesel	Serviceable
443642	Ruston Hornsby 4W DM	Serviceable
22928	Fowler 0-4-0DM Diesel	Undergoing Restoration

DIESEL MULTIPLE UNITS

Number/Description	Condition/Info	
M50980	DMU 108DMBS	Serviceable
M52054	DMU 108DMCL	Serviceable
M51947	DMU 108DMBS	Stored for Spares

Carriages and Wagons

The B&W have sets of BR MK1 carriages in Carmine and Cream as well as Chocolate and Cream. These plus a dining coach set in Chocolate and Cream are all in regular use. A few stored and many serviceable wagons can also be seen on the line including five BR 13T Clay Hoods and various brake vans.

*Breaking out into the open as it climbs past Charlie's Gate on its way back to Bodmin General from Bodmin Parkway was another special visitor during 2012. The Great Western Society's unique GWR Steam Railmotor **No.93**. 12 October 2012.*

*A little further along at Charlie's Gate, GWR Class 2-6-2 Prairie Tank **No.5552** pulls a rake of three carmine and cream carriages towards Bodmin General. 10 April 2011.*

*After Charlie's Gate the line runs alongside the main A38 for a short while then passes under it, but still climbing as it heads north-west. Once again we see the GWR Class 2-8-0 Tank **No.4247** in action. Here it is working hard as it tackles the climb to Colesloggett Halt with five carriages. 11 March 2012.*

*Prairie Tank **No.5552** reaches Colesloggett Halt in a cloud of smoke and steam and passes without stopping. Owing to the steep gradient on the line here, trains only stop on the outward-bound journey from Bodmin General to Bodmin Parkway. 31 December 2011.*

Right: *Bodmin and Wenford resident ex-GWR 0-6-0 Pannier Tank **No.6435** pilots an ex-GWR Side Tank (Possibly **No.5552**) still climbing towards Bodmin General as they pass under Fletchers Bridge at Turfdown. 26 June 2011.*

Homeward-bound GWR Class 2-8-0 Side Tank **No.4247** *is framed beautifully as it passes under the A38 bridge climbing its way from Colesloggett Halt to Bodmin General. 7 September 2012.*

Another 'double header', this time it's the home based Beattie 2-4-0 Well Tank **No.30587** *piloting the Drummond 4-4-0 T9* **No.30120** *as the train passes Quarry Curve just before the bridge near Walker Lines Industrial Estate. 10 April 2011.*

*On its first outing away from the Isle of Wight for many a decade, visiting 0-4-4 **Calbourne No.24** pilots Beattie Well Tank **No.30587** past the Walker Lines Sidings on the last part of our journey from Bodmin Parkway to Bodmin General Station. 21 April 2012.*

*Resident ex-GWR 0-6-0 Pannier Tank **No.6435** enters Bodmin General Station, completing our photographic journey from the southern terminus at Bodmin Parkway. The T9 4-4-0 Greyhound **No.30120** in the background is manoeuvring to take on water from the tower. 3 January 2011.*

Left: *Visiting LSWR Beattie 2-4-0WT **No.30585** with the last service of the day from Colesloggett Halt during the Bodmin and Wenford Cornish Branch Line Winter Steam Up weekend. The sunset adds a warm glow to the sky as the train passes under Beacon Road Bridge entering Bodmin General Station from the south. 3 January 2011.*

We now move to Bodmin and Wenford's northernmost terminus at Boscarne Junction to journey back along the line to Bodmin General. Ex-GWR Class 2-8-0 Tank **No.4247** *is seen 'running around' its train at Boscarne Junction, a station in a very picturesque location. The cycle track on the right of this picture has been built on the trackbed of the line which once ran to the quarries at Wenfordbridge. 18 July 2012.*

*Having just left Boscarne Junction, the ex-LSWR Class 2-4-0 Beattie Well Tank **No.30587** is about to cross the River Camel on its way back to Bodmin General pulling a demonstration goods train during the railway's September Steam Gala & Real Ale Festival. 7 September 2012.*

*Just before entering Bodmin General Station, GWR Class 0-6-0 Pannier Tank **No.6435** is captured on Checkrail Curve. 21 June 2011.*

*Left: Also taking part in the 2012 Steam Gala & Real Ale Festival, GWR 78xx Class 4-6-0 **No.7812 Erlestoke Manor** charges through Westheath on the long climb back towards Bodmin General Station. 7 September 2012.*

The end of our photographic journey along both lines of the Bodmin and Wenford Railway leaves us at rest at the main terminus at Bodmin General Station. Seen here, ex-GWR Class 2-8-0 Side Tank **No.4247** *sits alongside the platform during the 2012 Spring Steam Spectacular. 21 April 2012.*

DARTMOUTH STEAM RAILWAY

History of the Dartmouth Steam Railway

The branch line from Paignton to Kingswear on the south coast of Devon was originally opened in 1864 by the South Devon Railway and subsequently absorbed into the Great Western Railway during 1876.

Founded in 1960, the Dart Valley Railway PLC originally procured another railway – the Buckfastleigh to Totnes heritage line in1969 – but saw an opportunity to acquire this potentially more profitable Paignton to Kingswear branch line when it became threatened with closure under British Railways and the Beeching Report. In 1972 they were successful in buying the line beyond Goodrington as a heritage railway and started running train services in 1973.

The Dartmouth Steam Railway is unusual amongst heritage railways in that it is a fully commercial concern which does not rely on charitable donations or volunteer labour, with the exception of a few volunteers who help at the restored and re-opened Churston Station.

Although much had been preserved and restored, in order to open the railway for the public, DSR had to build the entirely new Queens Park Station adjacent to and sharing the site of the existing mainline Paignton Station on the old Park Sidings. During the winter of 2011 Queens Park Station saw massive investment to create a Great Western-style station but meeting modern visitor expectations and also to bring it up to the latest standards with regard to health and safety and access regulations.

Instead of pandering to the wishes of those who would have their steam experience historically accurate *exactly* as it was in some period of BR or GWR ownership, the Dartmouth Steam Railway chose to provide the steam experience with minor changes focused to provide greater family appeal. For example, all of the carriages now have names and so do the engines. Although many purists may well frown, it is difficult to deny the positive effect this approach has had on the majority of visitors.

This heritage railway still has a mainline connection and steam charter trains are frequent visitors on the line throughout the summer season. Because the DSR including all its signalling has been brought fully up to main line standards, it is also able to carry Britain's largest and heaviest locomotives.

Dartmouth Steam Railway's own ex-GWR 2-8-0 Tank locomotive **Hercules No.4277** *is captured in the late afternoon sunshine at Paignton Queens Park Station, just after arriving back from Kingswear. 15 April 2011.*

DSR acquired two river boat companies to complement the rail services and in 1999, the merged businesses became the Dartmouth Steam Railway & River Boat Company.

Website links:

- Further information on the Dartmouth Steam & Railway River Boat Company can be obtained from their website – *www.dartmouthrailriver.co.uk*

Track Layout and Stations

The Dartmouth Steam Railway is 7 miles in length and runs along some of the most beautiful scenery in England. Starting from Queens Park Station, the line heads south into Goodrington Sands Halt which is shared with Network Rail mainline trains. The line goes on to hug the dramatic English Riviera coastline, crossing two spectacular viaducts near Broadsands before climbing westwards into Churston Station.

Leaving Churston, the line meanders through gladed valleys towards Greenway Halt where passengers can alight for Greenway House, after which the line immediately drops through a long steep tunnel emerging to cross Greenway viaduct with a wonderful view of the River Dart. Heading southward once more the line weaves its way along the edge of the picturesque Dart estuary and into its riverside terminus beside the ferry crossing in Kingswear. On the return journey the steam engines can be heard working very hard as they climb back toward and through the Greenway tunnel heading for Churston.

Queens Park Station: In 2012 Dartmouth Steam Railway spent £1.6 million completely refurbishing Queens Park into a modern interpretation of a Great Western Railway station as their 'shiny new gateway to The Golden Age of Steam'. Situated in the centre of Paignton and 10 minutes walk from the seafront, it physically adjoins the mainline station but both lines are completely separated by fencing. The station

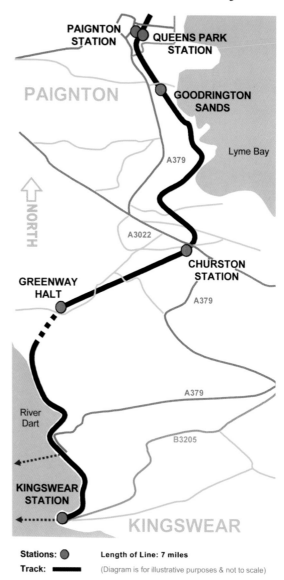

Dartmouth Steam Railway

PAIGNTON STATION

QUEENS PARK STATION

PAIGNTON

GOODRINGTON SANDS

Lyme Bay

A379

NORTH

A3022

CHURSTON STATION

GREENWAY HALT

A379

A379

River Dart

B3205

KINGSWEAR STATION

KINGSWEAR

Stations: ●   Length of Line: **7 miles**

Track: ▬▬   (Diagram is for illustrative purposes & not to scale)

has all the facilities one would expect from a modern venue, including a shopping area, restaurant and toilets. There is an adjacent bus depot and many nearby car parks.

Goodrington Sands Halt: Co-used by mainline rail and the heritage line, this halt is now a fairly barren station, but located very close to Goodrington beach and Water Park. There is a large car park nearby.

Churston Station: This restored GWR station stands on the A3022 main road to Brixham and was originally opened for passengers in 1861 (as Brixham Road) but was by-passed by BR in 1967.

Dartmouth Steam Railway installed a locomotive turntable at this station in 1981, which is now regularly put to good use on incoming steam charter specials.

Churston Station is also home to the railway's coachworks and locomotive engineering workshops and continues to expand. Currently under discussion is the possibility of running mainline rail 'Riviera Line' services from here to Exmouth.

Greenway Halt: This brand new halt was opened in 2012 to provide rail access (via a short walk) to the former summer residence of Agatha Christie at Greenway House. It is not possible for all trains to stop at Greenway Halt on the return journey from Kingswear, so it is wise to check the timetable carefully.

Kingswear Station: Located on the edge of the River Dart, this historic station is the southern terminus of the Dartmouth Steam Railway and was originally opened in 1864. The station has an unusual extended canopy which also covers the tracks as a train shed.

An impressive looking 'period signal box' was built opposite the main platform in 2011 but it actually houses railway offices. The second platform track was reinstated in 1976 and points are controlled by the engine crews using local ground frames. The station has a café, toilets, a ticket office and visitor centre. The large nearby car park was built on the site of the old goods sidings.

As Kingswear Station was the rail terminal for Dartmouth (across the estuary) there are adjacent foot passenger and car ferry terminals for those wishing to cross the river. Interestingly, the GWR station building in Dartmouth (now a café) sold tickets and took parcels, but uniquely never had tracks or trains.

*The first train of the day, ex-GWR Manor Class 4-6-0 **Lydham Manor No.7827** reverses away from Goodrington Sands Station above a colourful row of beach huts as it heads south towards Churston. 30 May 2013.*

In British Rail Black since her major overhaul in 2011, **Lydham Manor No.7827** *an ex-GWR Manor Class 4-6-0 locomotive owned and restored by the Dartmouth Steam Railway, is seen here heading south passing Waterside Cove shortly after leaving Goodrington. 8 June*

Dartmouth Steam Railway typical 'standard' daily timetable

Shown below is an example DSR daily timetable. Although the times are typical, they should not be taken literally as times may be adjusted from season to season as needs change. However it does give an idea of the frequency of trains and travel times between stations on a normal service day.

BLUE TIMETABLE (All steam)

PAIGNTON QUEENS PARK	10.30	11.15	12.15	13.00	14.15	15.15	16.15
GOODRINGTON	10.35	11.20	12.20	13.05	14.20	15.20	16.20
CHURSTON	10.45	11.30	12.30	13.15	14.30	15.30	16.30
GREENWAY HALT	10.50	11.35	12.35	13.20	14.35	15.35	16.35
KINGSWEAR	11.00	11.45	12.45	13.30	14.45	15.45	16.45
KINGSWEAR	11.15	12.15	13.00	14.15	15.15	16.15	17.00
GREENWAY HALT	11.25	12.25	13.10	x	x	x	x
CHURSTON	11.30	12.30	13.15	14.30	15.30	16.30	17.15
GOODRINGTON SANDS	11.40	12.40	13.25	14.40	15.40	16.40	17.25
PAIGNTON QUEENS PARK	11.45	12.45	13.30	14.45	15.45	16.45	17.30

NOTE: Not all trains stop at Greenway Halt on the return journey from Kingswear.

During peak season and on special galas, the Dartmouth Steam Railway runs a far busier schedule than that shown above, frequently nine trains each way. Conversely during a large part of the off-peak season, there may well be typically only four trains each way.

LOCOMOTIVES ON THE DARTMOUTH STEAM RAILWAY   Circa 2012/2013

The list below is only intended as a guide to stock recently associated with the line.

STEAM LOCOMOTIVES

Number/Description	Condition/Info	
4277 *Hercules*	GWR 4200 Class 2-8-0T	Serviceable
5239 *Goliath*	GWR 5205 Class 2-8-0T	
7827 *Lydham Manor*	GWR 7800 Class 4-6-0	Serviceable
75014 *Braveheart*	BR standard Class 4-6-0	

The **Devon Belle** observation car allows passengers excellent panoramic views as the line winds its way around Salter Cove on the English Riviera, heading towards Churston Station from Goodrington Sands. 8 June 2012.

Two luxury Pullman observation cars have been preserved from the 1960s and both run regularly on south west heritage railways, this one on the DSR and the other at Swanage.

DIESEL LOCOMOTIVES

Number/Description	Condition/Info
D7535 *Mercury*	BR Class 25 Bo-Bo
D2192 *Titan*	BR Class 03 0-6-0 shunter
D3014 *Samson*	BR Class 08 0-6-0 shunter

Carriages and Wagons

The railway currently has a fleet of 20 coaches each adorned with a girl's name, a Pullman observation saloon and a refurbished carriage used as a Brunel exhibit at Kingswear Station.

The railway occasionally runs a selection of freight wagons on special events. Many are just for show and stored in sidings although some do get used for maintenance and engineering work along the line.

DSR ran a fabulous, if little advertised, Steam Gala during 2012, which included this long demonstration goods train. 8 June 2012.

This view across Saltern Cove as **Lydham Manor No.7827** *heads south for the turntable at Churston, clearly shows the proximity of the Dartmouth Steam Railway to this dramatic and rugged coastline. 5 March 2013.*

Right: *GWR 2-8-0T Class* **7F Hercules No.4277*** *leads nine carriages past Shell Cove, pulling the train northwards from Churston to Paignton. 8 June 2012.*

* *Tank engine No.4277 was one of the 4200 Class of locomotives originally built in 1920 at the Great Western Railway's Swindon Works and has been with Dartmouth Steam Railway since 2008.*

Whilst visiting the Dartmouth Steam Railway during the 2012 summer season, ex-GWR 4-6-0 Hall Class locomotive **No.4936 Kinlet Hall**, *draws the* **Devon Belle** *observation car past Broadsands on route from Churston to Paignton. 8 June 2012.*

Right: *Seen here crossing Broadsands Viaduct – the first of three viaducts encountered along the journey from Paignton to Kingswear – GWR 2-8-0 Tank* **No.4277 Hercules** *heads south towards Churston. 15 April 2012.*

*Another DSR-owned ex-GWR 2-8-0 Tank locomotive on Broadsands Viaduct. This time it's **Goliath No.5239** heading south to Churston during summer. 24 August 2011.*

GWR 2-8-0 Tank locomotive **Goliath No.5239** *reaches the second viaduct along the line from Paignton to Kingswear. The magnificent nine arch, 85 feet high, 116 yard long Hookhills Viaduct is situated between Broadsands and Galmpton just before the line reaches Churston Station. 24 August 2011.*

Approximately half way along our journey is Churston Station. Here the doubled track allows trains to pass, therefore enabling a two train running timetable during the busy peak season. 24 August 2011.

*Right: After Churston Station the line drops through a cutting and meanders towards Greenway Halt. GWR 2-8-0T **Hercules No.4277** is captured working hard on its way back northward to Churston from Greenway. 24 August 2011.*

*Dartmouth Steam Railway's ex-GWR 2-8-0T **Goliath No.5239** heads south past Brim Hill to Greenway Halt. 24 August 2011.*

*Standing at the recently opened Greenway Halt, GWR Manor Class 4-6-0 **Lydham Manor No.7827** prepares to exit down through Greenway Tunnel before crossing the third viaduct on this picturesque line. 25 July 2012.*

Left: *Ex-GWR 4-6-0 **Lydham Manor No.7827** approaches the newly-built Greenway Halt, opened in 2012. 25 July 2012.*

Continuing our photographic journey after crossing Greenway Viaduct we break out onto the banks of the River Dart. Seen here approaching the Kingswear-Dartmouth Higher Ferry slipway is ex-GWR 2-8-0T **No.4277 Hercules** *returning from Kingswear. 5 April 2013.*

Left: *Still heading south-west after exiting Greeway Tunnel,* **Lydham Manor** *crosses the picturesque Greenway Viaduct which overlooks the River Dart. 26 April 2013.*

*Originally built in 1923, ex-GWR 2-8-0 Tank locomotive **Goliath No.5239** is captured hauling a summer train shortly before reaching the Kingswear terminus. 24 August 2011.*

Right: *Mainline charter trains also frequent the DSR's heritage rails throughout the year and here ex-Southern Region **No.34046 Braunton**, a rebuilt Westcountry Class Pacific, is seen hauling the Torbay Express on the return journey from Kingswear. 1 September 2013.*

As trains cross Waterhead Creek before entering Kingswear Station the observation car really comes into its own, providing tremendous all round views of the Dart estuary and Britannia Royal Naval College situated on the hill above the town. 28 August 2011.

*Viewed from just above the access foot-bridge at Kingswear Station, ex-GWR Tank locomotive **No.4277 Hercules** arrives easing its seven coach train over a level crossing and into the long curved main platform. 5 April 2013.*

*The end of the line: locomotive **No.7827 Lydham Manor** proudly sits on view at Dartmouth Steam Railway's southern terminus at Kingswear Station in South Devon. Here many passengers disembark and catch the adjacent ferry to Dartmouth. Note the extended canopy which can provide cover for locomotives. 25 July 2012.*

SOUTH DEVON RAILWAY

History of the South Devon Railway

The South Devon Railway is based at its Buckfastleigh Station terminus. From there the line runs south-west along a beautiful stretch of the River Dart to the market town of Totnes. Built in 1872 by the Buckfastleigh, Totnes and South Devon Railway (which subsequently amalgamated into the Great Western Railway during 1876), the line originally ran from Ashburton via Buckfastleigh to Totnes. The line was nationalised in 1948 and ten years later saw its last passenger train well before the 'Beeching Axe' cut so many of the UK's branch lines for British Rail in the '60s. The final goods train ran in 1962.

Dart Valley Railway PLC was founded in the early 1960s with the intention of acquiring and running this line as a commercial heritage railway. The first rolling stock arrived in 1965 and the newly named Dart Valley Railway was officially reopened by the notorious Dr Beeching himself in 1969.

Volunteers kept the railway in good working order until it opened, then helped with operations and eventually formed The South Devon Railway Trust charity, which took over the running of the loss-making line in 1991 and renamed it the South Devon Railway. By 2000, the Trust began negotiations to purchase the line from the Dart Valley Railway PLC who were now preoccupied running their more profitable Dartmouth Steam Railway and the whole transaction process was finally completed in 2010. Sadly due to the widening of the A38 in 1971, the section from Buckfastleigh to Ashburton was lost.

One of the most difficult hurdles for the preserved South Devon Railway to overcome and to ensure success, was its very tenuous link with the town of Totnes. Although originally built as a branch line which joined the mainline just before crossing the River Dart and terminating at Totnes mainline station, this option was no longer available in preservation. So the single track line ended only a few hundred metres from Totnes, but having no land access whatsoever, the SDR was effectively cut off from its potentially most lucrative source of custom. However, land adjacent to the Totnes end of the line was acquired in 1977 which allowed a 'run around loop' for the engine to be constructed and shortly after a

Ex-GWR 0-6-0 Pannier Tank **No.6430** *visiting from the Llangollen Railway for the Military Gala weekend, prepares to leave the South Devon Railway terminus at Buckfastleigh Station on a wet afternoon. 7 July 2012.*

platform was built. This new station was originally called Totnes Riverside but to avoid confusion was soon renamed Littlehempston Riverside. In 1993 a footbridge was built to cross the river finally connecting the terminus with the town and the station was then renamed as Totnes Littlehempston.

Some 500 members of the *South Devon Railway Association* (a volunteer support body with around 2500 members in total) actively assist with the day to day running of the SDR railway. They also provide financial support to the *South Devon Railway Trust* charity which is responsible for operating the railway.

Since 1991 the railway has expanded enormously. A passing loop was built near Staverton Station which enabled a two train running system during busy periods. The station buildings at Totnes Littlehempston have been completed and two historic GWR signal boxes have also been re-erected on the line. *South Devon Railway Engineering*, a flourishing engineering business for the repair and maintenance of locomotives and rolling stock, has also been established at Buckfastleigh.

Website links:
- Further information on the South Devon Railway (SDR) can be obtained from their website – *www.southdevonrailway.co.uk*
- Further information about the South Devon Railway Association (SDRA) can be obtained from their website – *www.southdevonrailwayassociation.org*
- Further information about the South Devon Railway Engineering can be obtained from their website – *www.southdevonrailwayengineering.co.uk*

Track Layout and Stations

The South Devon Railway heritage line is just under 7 miles in length and closely hugs the picturesque fast-flowing River Dart which provides a scenic backdrop all the way from the highest point on the line at Buckfastleigh downriver to Totnes.

Upon leaving Buckfastleigh Station the line heads south-west passing almost immediately under an old road bridge, then shortly after crosses over the River Dart on the open-span Nursery Pool Bridge to remain on its left bank. Caddaford Curve where the A384 and railway almost touch is swiftly approached – this is a popular spot for photographers.

Approximately ten minutes from Buckfastleigh the A384 crosses both the river and the railway on the beautiful granite three-arch Riverford Bridge – also known as Hood Bridge. Again, this is another location highly favoured by photographers.

Situated approximately half way, Staverton Station is the only intermediate station on the line. Almost unchanged for a 100 years it is a real slice of history. Directly adjacent is an old mill (recently converted to multiple dwellings) and a very long narrow medieval bridge with much attached folklore.

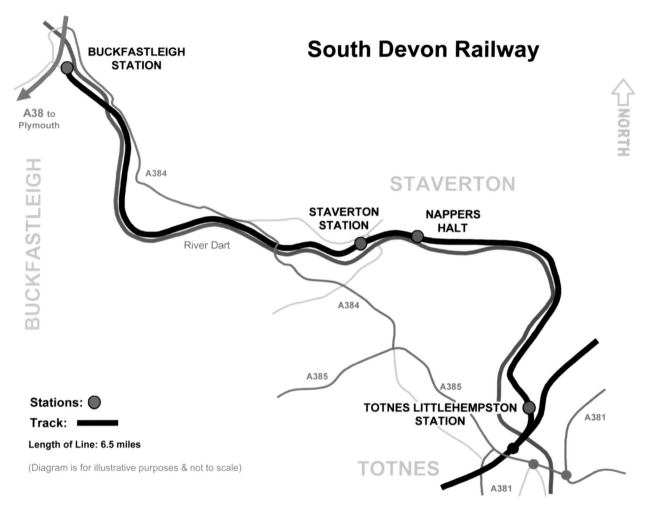

South Devon Railway

BUCKFASTLEIGH
STATION

A38 to
Plymouth

NORTH

A384

BUCKFASTLEIGH

STAVERTON

STAVERTON
STATION

NAPPERS
HALT

River Dart

A384

A385

A385

TOTNES LITTLEHEMPSTON
STATION

A381

Stations: ⬤

Track: ▬▬▬▬

Length of Line: 6.5 miles

(Diagram is for illustrative purposes & not to scale)

TOTNES

A381

Leaving Staverton through a level crossing, the line is embraced by deciduous trees before opening out at Nappers Halt near Staverton village – a very tiny request stop! Finally, the line edges slightly away from the River Dart on the approach to its riverside terminus, the station of Totnes Littlehempston.

*South Devon Railway's own GWR 0-6-0 **No.3205**, resplendent in late afternoon sunlight, exits Buckfastleigh Station for Totnes from under the footbridge crossing at the southern end of the terminus, during an end of season half price weekend. 2 November 2013.*

*Shortly after leaving Buckfastleigh Station heading south towards Staverton with a rake of Carmine and Cream carriages, South Devon Railway's ex-GWR 2-6-2 Prairie Tank **No.5526** crosses Nursery Pool Bridge on the River Dart during the popular SDR Half Price Weekend. 29 October 2011.*

Buckfastleigh Station: Kept in the style of how it would have been in the 1870s, this station is the headquarters of the South Devon Railway and also the new northern terminus since the Ashburton link was severed in 1971. The goods shed, now converted into a railway museum, houses *Tiny*, the last remaining Brunel broad gauge locomotive.

There are disabled access, toilets, a gift shop, model shop and restaurant plus landscaped gardens with a miniature ride-on railway and picnic area. The steam locomotive depot and workshops have a public viewing area and a large car park sited on the old goods sidings is shared with Dartmoor Otters/Butterfly Farm.

Staverton Station: A classic example of a typical small GWR station, Staverton is run and maintained by members of the Staverton Preservation Group. Built to serve the nearby village and mill, it is the only intermediate station on the branch line and has remained largely unchanged for over a 100 years. The original signal box was rescued from a garden when the line was reopened under preservation and is now situated at the platform end beside the traditional wooden level crossing gates. There are toilets and ample parking at this station.

Nappers Halt: Opened by the South Devon Railway Trust, this un-advertised request stop is at ground level and at around 5 metres long is possibly one of the smallest railway halts anywhere in the world. It actually provides the opportunity to 'flag down' a steam train!

Totnes Littlehempston: This relatively new station (originally called Totnes Riverside) was built from scratch to provide a terminus at the Totnes end of the heritage line when line access to the Totnes mainline station was no longer permitted. Although just across the river, Totnes Littlehempston originally had no access to the town but is now well connected via a footbridge and also a ferry when the tide is in!

Volunteers created this award-winning period station using rescued railway buildings and artefacts from many derelict lines around the South West. There is a railway enthusiast's memorabilia/bookshop housed in an historic GWR Monster covered wagon on platform 2 and also an indoor/outdoor buffet area sited immediately across the tracks near the signal box and towards the adjacent Rare Breeds farm.

This station is situated very close to the mainline station and has a rail connection (via a padlocked gate) which permits special trains to run directly between the SDR heritage line and the national rail network.

*Seen here in heavy rain passing over a river access bridge near Caddaford Curve, the visiting BR Standard Class 4MT 2-6-4 Tank **No.80072**, pilots South Devon Railway's GWR Collet 0-6-0 **No.3205**, with a double header from Totnes to Buckfastleigh on a typically wet Easter Monday. 9 April 2012.*

South Devon Railway typical 'off-peak' daily timetable

Shown overleaf is an example SDR daily timetable. Although the times are typical, they should not be taken literally as times may be adjusted from season to season as needs change. However it does give an idea of the frequency of trains on a quiet day and also travel times between stations.

RED TIMETABLE (Basic service, single train running.)					
		a.m.	p.m.	p.m.	p.m.
BUCKFASTLEIGH	Depart	**10.45**	**12.15**	**2.15**	**3.45**
STAVERTON	Depart	11.00	12.30	2.30	4.00
TOTNES-LITTLEHEMPSTON	Arrive	11.15	12.45	2.45	4.15
		a.m.	p.m.	p.m.	p.m.
TOTNES-LITTLEHEMPSTON	Depart	11.30	1.00	3.00	4.30
STAVERTON	Depart	11.40	1.10	3.10	4.40
BUCKFASTLEIGH	Arrive	**12.00**	**1.30**	**3.30**	**5.00**

During peak times and on special galas a two train running system is put into operation on the South Devon Railway which more than doubles the number of trains running daily. Normally nine trains run each way on their blue peak timetable and even more during some galas. The SDR also put on a very large number of other family events, plus frequent evening and late night specials, for which times are always posted separately on their website: *www.southdevonrailway.co.uk*

LOCOMOTIVES ON THE SOUTH DEVON RAILWAY   Circa 2012/2013

The list below is only intended as a guide to stock recently associated with the line.

STEAM LOCOMOTIVES

Number/Description		Condition/Info
1369	GWR 1366 Class 0-6-0PT	Serviceable
3205	GWR 2251 Class 0-6-0	Serviceable
3803	GWR 2884 Class2-8-0	Away in Service
4920	*Dumbleton Hall* GWR 4-6-0	Awaiting Overhaul
5526	GWR 4575 Class 2-6-2T	Awaiting Overhaul
5786	GWR 57XX Class 0-6-0PT	Out of Service
1420	GWR 14XX Class0-4-2T	Out of Service
6412	GWR 64xx Class 0-6-0PT	Out of Service

Earl of Berkely*, a 4-4-0 Earl Class locomotive **No.9017** passing one of the most popular locations for photographers on the South Devon Railway. Seen here heading south on Caddaford Curve, where the River Dart, railway and Buckfastleigh to Totnes main road all come together. Nicknamed Dukedog owing to the Earl class being built from parts originally created for the preceding 'Duke' and 'Bulldog' class locomotives, 9017 which is usually on the Bluebell Railway, was another visitor to the South Devon line. This time for the Cambrian Gala. 23 April 2011.*

Glendower	WD Austerity Class 0-6-0ST		Undergoing Overhaul
1 *Ashley*	Peckett 0-4-0ST		On Display
Lady Angela	Peckett 0-4-0ST		Recently Restored
47 *Carnarvon*	Kitson 0-6-0ST		On Display
Lee Moor No2	4'6" Gauge 0-4-0ST		On Display
151 *Tiny*	SDR 0-4-0VB (Broad Guage)		On Display

INTERNAL COMBUSTION LOCOMOTIVES

Number	Class	Type	Builder/Propulsion Method
D402/50002	Class 50	Co Co	English Electric - Diesel Electric
D6501/33002	Class 33	Bo Bo	B.R.C.W. Sulzer Diesel Electric
D 8110/20110	Class 20	Bo Bo	English Electric - Diesel Electric
D3721/09010	Class 09	0-6-0DE	English Electric - Diesel Electric
418793 *Dusty*		0-4-0DH	Ruston - Diesel Hydraulic
L052 *Yorky*		0-6-0DE	Yorkshire Engine - Diesel Electric
MFP4		0-4-0	Fowler - Diesel Mechanical
D2246/11216	Class 04	0-6-0DM	R Stephenson & Hawthorn - Diesel Mech.
D6737/37037 *Loch Treig*	Class 37	Co Co	English Electric - Diesel Electric
W55000	Class 121		Single Unit Diesel Mechanical Unit
D7541/25191	Class 25	Bo Bo	BR Crewe 1966
D7612/25262	Class 25	Bo Bo	BR Crewe 1966
DR73274	07	07	Plasser & Theurer
DR98210	TRAMM	TRAMM	Plasser & Theurer

Carriages and Wagons

The South Devon Railway has a large collection of historic GWR and BR rolling stock which includes twenty nine passenger carrying vehicles and full brake coaches. Many are already in regular use and others are gradually being returned to working condition. The intention is to have complete sets of the following: Chocolate and Cream Mark I carriage set, Crimson and Cream Mark I set, Great Western set, Auto Train, High capacity 'Branch Line' set, Victorian set for special occasions and a Dining Train.

During recent years, SDR has also built up an interesting cross section of old freight wagons which includes GWR wagons, BR wagons, LMS, LNER and private owner wagons, plus Wickham Trolleys.

*Ex GWR 0-6-0 Pannier Tank **No.6430** at Caddaford Curve heading for Staverton. 8 July 2012.*

*Another photograph taken at Caddaford Curve and showing why it is such a popular location. This time a north-bound train being pulled by South Devon Railway's own GWR 0-6-0 **No.3205** is seen with a head of steam approaching the curve from the direction of Stretchford and heading towards Buckfastleigh. 29 October 2011.*

Up close and personal at Riverford Bridge – Jinty **No.47406** pulls a late afternoon train north towards Buckfastleigh under the A384 at Riverford. Nicknamed Jinty, over four hundred of these LMS Fowler Class 3F 0-6-0 Tank locomotives were produced and this one – normally based on the Great Central Railway – was visiting the South Devon Railway during for the Cambrian Gala. 23 April 2011.

Left: *Continuing our photographic journey down the line from Buckfastleigh to Totnes, we next reach Riverford Bridge (also referred to locally as Hood Bridge), which is another outstandingly picturesque section of the line. Summer or winter, passengers can usually see keen photographers lining the opposite bank of the river as they travel along this part of their journey. Once again Dukedog* **No.9017** *is seen heading south towards the bridge. 23 April 2011.*

*Looking upstream from Riverford on a rainy summer day. South Devon Railway's
ex-GWR 0-6-0 Pannier Tank **No.1369** heads south towards Staverton. 17 June 2011.*

*Visiting GWR 0-6-0 Pannier Tank **No.6430** approaches Staverton Station from Buckfastleigh in the early afternoon during the Military Gala weekend. 8 July 2012.*

*Ex-GWR 4575 Class Small Prairie Tank **No.5542** is a frequent visitor to the South Devon Railway. It is seen here awaiting departure at Staverton Station for Totnes. This original Staverton signal box had been used as a shed in a nearby garden after line closure but was rescued, fully restored and reinstated. 3 June 2012.*

*Leaving Staverton Station to continue towards Totnes, the line immediately exits the station through a wooden gated level crossing. The gates are controlled manually by the signal box operator. Here Dukedog **No.9017** is seen pulling away in the late morning sunshine. 23 April 2011.*

*SDR's ex-GWR 0-6-0 Pannier Tank **No.1369** is seen approaching the request stop at Nappers Halt just before Staverton. At around 5 metres long it is possibly one of the smallest railway halts anywhere in the world. 25 March 2012.*

*Once again GWR **No.3205** is seen returning from Totnes, this time caught
working hard towards Woodville Water Board Crossing shortly after
leaving Totnes Station heading for Buckfastleigh. 29 October 2011.*

Left: *South Devon Railway's trusty GWR 0-6-0 tender engine **No.3205**
is seen further down the line from Nappers Halt, as it passes along the
River Dart at Dartington on its way back from Totnes. 8 April 2012.*

*Visiting GWR Pannier Tank **No.6430** fitted with Autocoach passes the station signal box as it enters the South Devon Railway's southern terminus at Totnes. Autocoaches are carriages fitted out with a driving position and a set of controls, which allows operation of the train from either the engine cab or the coach, hence saving time as there is no need for engines to 'run around' their coaches before starting return journeys. 26 July 2012.*

*The end of the line, our journey from Buckfastleigh finally terminates at Totnes Littlehempston Station. On the right of the picture, the Network Rail mainline tracks can be seen running almost parallel to the station. The two rail networks are still linked, but access either way needs special permission and then via a padlocked gate. Families wait for the GWR 0-6-0 Pannier Tank **No.6430** to come to a halt before embarking. 8 July 2012.*

*A wonderful view from the trackside restaurant as GWR 0-6-0 **No.3205** couples up to the carriages and makes ready to leave Totnes Littlehempston riverside station for the return journey to Buckfastleigh. 2 August 2012.*

SWANAGE RAILWAY

History of the Swanage Railway

In 1885, after overcoming many years of objections from the residents of Wareham regarding the proposed route of what is now the Swanage Heritage Railway, The London & South Western Railway Company opened the Swanage Station in the Purbeck district of Dorset to the public.

However, there were far more objections when British Rail first proposed closing the line eighty-one years later! The last steam train – an especially organised railtour – ran on the Swanage branch in June 1967. BR kept a spartan, mainly railcar service, running for a few more years yet the line struggled on despite being stripped and ransacked. The death knell finally came on New Year's Day 1972.

Despite the best efforts of the Isle of Purbeck Preservation Group and then the newly formed Swanage Railway Society, preservation efforts failed. This was largely due to the impossible £126,500 that British Rail were demanding for the 7 miles of track between Swanage and Furzebrook. Track lifting commenced the following July from the Swanage end and in just seven weeks the line was gone.

However, the Swanage Railway Society never gave up and after three years and a referendum among the people of Swanage, the councils finally agreed to lease back the trackbed in 1975. Sadly by that time the once proud Swanage and Corfe Stations had both gone to rack and ruin and not many would have thought there was any chance of bringing the line back to life.

However from little acorns...

It took until 1980 for the track to be re-laid the short distance from the engine shed at Northbrook Road Bridge back into the main platform at Swanage. Up until 1984 a small saddle tank steam locomotive ran on this short section, after which its run was extended a further mile due to the track having been re-laid to Herston where a simple wooden halt had been built which could accept passenger trains.

A major obstacle was eliminated in 1986 when the county council voted to allow Corfe Castle Station to be used as a railway and not be demolished for a by-pass!

By 1987 the track had reached a further 3 miles to Harmon's Cross where the first new station in Dorset for more than 50 years was built. It received the first public train in 1989.

1991 must have been the most bitter-sweet year ever for the Swanage Railway Company and the hundreds of willing volunteers when the track finally reached Corfe Castle at the very time a financial crisis all but forced bankruptcy. Despite volunteers having to eliminate a nearly half million pound debt, track laying work continued and, in April 1992, reached the site where Norden Station and the Park and Ride were built. Corfe Castle Station was finally opened for public service trains from Swanage in 1995.

Track laying continued and there is now, albeit through padlocked gates, a full connection between the Swanage Railway and the mainline. The first steam locomotive from Wareham to Swanage in forty years finally ran in 2007. It had taken British Rail seven weeks to lift the 6.5 miles of track and Swanage Railway volunteers thirty years to re-lay them!

From April to October, the Swanage Railway currently runs a comprehensive daily service timetable, reduced to week-ends only during November and March. In addition, they also run, cater for and support many special and local events, for families, the local community and, of course, rail enthusiasts – even through the depths of mid winter. The Park and Ride facilities at Norden station have been increased to support the overwhelming success of the SR ventures.

The Swanage Railway Company Ltd is responsible for the day to day operation of the Swanage Railway and all volunteers working on the railway are expected to comply with the Company's policies and procedures in the same way as the Company's employees.

The Swanage Railway Trust was formed as a charity with the aims of preserving the heritage of the local railway and re-establishing a link to the national rail network. A trading subsidiary (the Swanage Railway Company) operates the trains and is responsible for day to day management of the railway.

Website links:
- Further information on the Swanage Railway Company Ltd can be obtained from their website – *www.swanagerailway.co.uk*
- Further information about the Swanage Railway Trust can be obtained from their website – *www.swanagerailwaytrust.org.uk*

*Our photographic journey along the Swanage Railway starts from its current northern terminus at Norden Station and heads towards Swanage. Ex-GWR 0-6-2 Tank **No.6695** exits the station under the dilapidated bridge which is a remnant from the adjacent and long defunct narrow gauge Norden clay works tramway. 2 August 2011.*

*Swanage Railway's ex-Southern Region rebuilt West Country Class 4-6-2 **Eddystone** No.34028 on the approach to Norden Station returning from Corfe Castle Station. The iconic ruins of Corfe Castle can be seen along much of the first half of the route. 7 April 2012.*

Track Layout and Stations

The Swanage Railway is currently 6 miles in length and follows the route of the original Purbeck branch line from Norden via Corfe Castle and Harman's Cross to Herston Halt and finally terminates at Swanage.

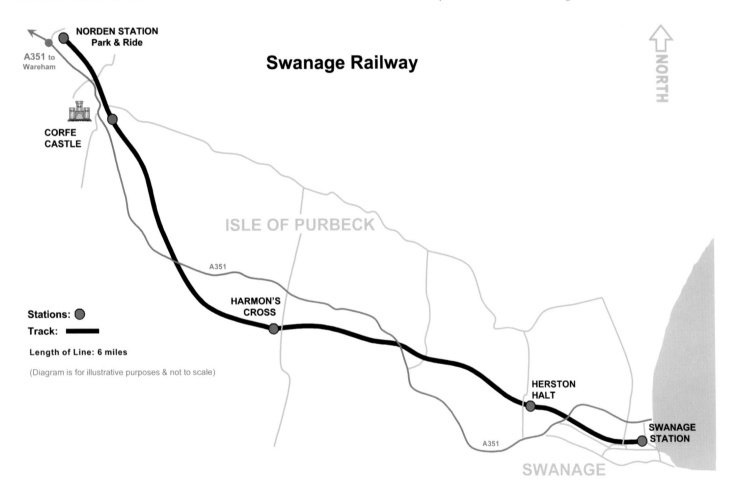

From Norden heading south-east, the elevated line crosses Norden Viaduct revealing fabulous views of the historic ruins of Corfe Castle before cutting through a short pass to Corfe Castle Station. The railway then continues largely elevated through open countryside providing long views of rolling Dorset farmland dotted with small woods. After Harmon's

Cross there are a few short cuttings and many elevated sections until reaching the terminus at Swanage which is superbly placed in the town centre and very close to both beach and harbour.

Swanage Station: This town centre station is the main terminus and home of the Swanage Railway Company since restoration started in 1976. Built in grey Purbeck stone it has two platform tracks situated either side of a single passenger platform, the longer of which has a run round loop. A viewing platform overlooks the nearby engine shed, turntable and coaling stage. Facilities include a buffet, railway shop, council operated toilets (not designated disabled) and a bus station. There are large town car parks nearby.

Herston Halt: Herston Halt is a simple wooden-platformed request stop which was opened nine years after a licence was received to occupy the Swanage site (Easter 1984). In 1997 the halt was adopted by the Royal Signals Corps who have supported general maintenance and larger capital projects ever since. In 2009 the original platform was replaced with an ex-Southern Railway structure.

Harman's Cross Station: The first completely new station to be built in Dorset for over fifty years. The whole station including platforms, buildings and signal box was created by Swanage Railway volunteers in 1989. Both platforms are accessed and connected via a long sloping path to a road bridge. A passing loop constructed in 1997 has made this the main crossing point for trains. There is a small charge for the limited space nearby car park.

Corfe Castle Station: This picturesque fully restored Southern Region station reopened in 1995. It is double tracked with twin platforms interconnected with a period iron footbridge. The station rests in the shadow of what is possibly the most famous castle ruin in southern England and is home to Swanage Railway's Museum. Toilet facilities are available.

Norden Station: This new station and its Park and Ride facility (ideal for Corfe Castle and Swanage) was built a half mile north of Corfe Castle village in 1995 at the location of the former exchange sidings, between the Swanage branch and the clay tramways. It is currently the line's north-west terminus. Facilities include the Norden Nest Buffet (open most operating days) toilets, plus a play and picnic area.

The Future

The Swanage Railway's aim is to fully restore the 11 miles of track from Swanage to Wareham and to re-establish a daily service which will connect with the mainline trains. Although trains can be exchanged between the Swanage Railway and Network Rail, currently this can only be done via a series of padlocked gates until signalling can be interfaced. In early 2013 the UK government announced a £1.5m grant to enable this work to proceed.

*Swanage Railway's Collett designed ex-GWR 5600 Class 0-6-2T **No.6695** pulling a rake of 'Southern' coaches across the viaduct over the B3351Studland road and approaching Corfe Castle Station from Norden. 30 July 2011.*

*High above the houses in the village of Corfe Castle, BR Standard Class 4 Mixed Traffic 2-6-4 Tank **No.80104** cruises over the Sandy Hill Lane road bridge preceeding the station. 30 July 2011.*

Swanage Railway typical 'standard' daily timetable

Shown below is an example Swanage railway daily timetable. Although the times are typical, they should not be taken literally as times may be adjusted from season to season as needs change. However it does give an idea of the frequency of trains and travel times between stations on a normal service day.

GREEN TIMETABLE (Example from 2013)

		Steam	Diesel	Steam	Diesel	Steam	Diesel	Steam	Diesel	Steam	Diesel	Steam	Diesel
SWANAGE	Depart	10:00	10:40	11:20	12:00	12:40	13:20	14:00	14:40	15:20	16:00	16:40	17:20
Herston**	Depart	**	**	**	**	**	**	**	**	**	**	**	**
Harmans Cross	Depart	10:10	10:50	11:30	12:10	12:50	13:30	14:10	14:50	15:30	16:10	16:50	17:30
Corfe Castle	Depart	10:20	11:00	11:40	12:20	13:00	13:40	14:20	15:00	15:40	16:20	17:00	17:40
NORDEN	Arrive	10:25	11:05	11:45	12:25	13:05	13:45	14:25	15:05	15:45	16:25	17:05	17:45

		Steam	Diesel	Steam	Diesel	Steam	Diesel	Steam	Diesel	Steam	Diesel	Steam	Diesel
NORDEN	Depart	10:40	11:20	12:00	12:40	13:20	14:00	14:40	15:20	16:00	16:40	17:20	18:00
Corfe Castle	Depart	10:42	11:22	12:02	12:42	13:22	14:02	14:42	15:22	16:02	16:42	17:22	18:02
Harmans Cross	Depart	10:52	11:32	12:12	12:52	13:32	14:12	14:52	15:32	16:12	16:52	17:32	18:12
Herston**	Depart	**	**	**	**	**	**	**	**	**	**	**	**
SWANAGE	Arrive	11:04	11:44	12:24	13:04	13:44	14:24	15:04	15:44	16:24	17:04	17:44	18:24

** Request stop for those wishing to get on and off the train at Herston Halt. Please advise our on board staff if you wish to get off at this stop. To join the train from Herston Halt, please give a clear hand signal to the driver.

In peak season, busy weekends and on special galas, the above timetable may be increased to 15 or more trains each way. During these events the locomotives in use are normally all steam until around 6pm then diesel units are operated to cover the late evening stints. There are also frequent special events run throughout the quiet winter months and especially at Christmas. Timetables for these are always posted well in advance on the Swanage Railway website: *www.swanagerailway.co.uk*

*The ruins of Corfe Castle dominate the skyline as the ex-British Railways Standard 2-6-4 Tank **No.80104** enters Corfe Castle Station from Norden. 24 July 2011.*

LOCOMOTIVES ON THE SWANAGE RAILWAY

The list below is only intended as a guide to stock recently associated with the line.

STEAM LOCOMOTIVES

Number/Description		Condition/Info
30053 LSWR 0-4-4T	Class M7	Serviceable
34028 *Eddystone*	SR 4-6-2 West Country Class	Serviceable
80104 BR 2-6-4T	Class 4MT	Serviceable
6695 GWR 0-6-2T	5600 Class	Serviceable
34070 *Manston*	SR 4-6-2 Battle of Britain Class	Serviceable
80078 BR 2-6-4T	Class 4MT	Awaiting Overhaul
34072 *257 Squadron*	SR 4-6-2 Battle of Britain Class	Awaiting Overhaul
34010 *Sidmouth*	SR 4-6-2 West Country Class	Awaiting Restoration
34053 *Sir Keith Park*	SR 4-6-2 Battle of Britain Class	Undergoing Restoration

DIESEL LOCOMOTIVES

Number/Description		Condition/Info
08436 BR 0-6-0	Class 08 (the Swanage shunter).	Serviceable
D3591 BR 0-6-0	Class 08	Serviceable
33111 BR Bo-Bo	Class 33 Crompton.	Serviceable
33012/D6515 BR Bo-Bo	Class 33 Crompton.	Serviceable
Fowler 0-4-0DM	Shunter May	Undergoing Restoration
D6552 (33034) BR Bo-Bo	Class 33 Crompton	Stored for Spares

DIESEL MULTIPLE UNITS

Number/Description	Condition/Info
BR Class 121 unit W55028 Bubble Car	Serviceable
BR Class 108 unit 51933+56504 Power Car 51933	Serviceable
BR Class 117 unit 51346+51388	Awaiting Overhaul
Trailer car 59516	Just Refurbished.

*Holidaymakers check the photos they have just taken of the home-based 1905-built ex-LSWR M7 Class 0-4-4 Tank locomotive **No.53** as it pulls to a halt in Corfe Castle Station. The prominent Victorian-style signal box on the down platform was officially opened in May 2012. 28 July 2012.*

Carriages and Wagons

The Swanage Railway Trust owns and is custodian of one of the country's most important collections of former Southern Railway coaches. However, the regular carriage sets on the Swanage Railway are currently BR Mk1's in Southern Region green. After a successful Heritage Coach Fund appeal, a Bulleid semi-open brake third was returned into service during 2012 and a Bulleid Corridor Composite coach could also be in service shortly when restoration is completed. Future plans for a unique Maunsell carriage set are also in place.

The Southern Catering Project Group also has a number of railway wagons stored on the Swanage Railway and maintains a comprehensive list of those on their website at *www.scpg.org.uk*

*Un-rebuilt Battle of Britain Class Light Pacific 4-6-2 **Manston No.34070**, passes under the platform footbridge at Corfe Castle Station on its arrival from Swanage. 24 July 2011.*

*Shortly after leaving Corfe Castle Station heading towards Swanage, the M7 Class 0-4-4 Tank **No.53** crosses over an access underpass leading to the Sandyhills Copse and Corfe Common. 25 May 2012.*

Moving further along the line ex-GWR 0-6-2 Tank **No.6695** passes through Corfe Common heading towards Townsend Bridge. The ruins of Corfe Castle are still prominent on the distant skyline. 3 July 2011.

Right: *Passing under Townsend Bridge, Battle of Britain Class Light Pacific 4-6-2* **Manston No.34070** *cruises towards Corfe Castle from Swanage with a rake of carriages resplendent in their Southern colours. 24 July 2011.*

*Still at Townsend Bridge we view a very unusual sight, visiting Port of Par twins **Alfred** and **Judy**, double head to tow a Diesel Railcar multiple unit from Swanage to the Norden Station Park and Ride during the Swanage Railway 2012 Autumn Grand Steam Gala. These unusually low 0-4-0 saddle tank locomotives were built by Bagnall for use under particularly low bridges at Par harbour in Cornwall. 9 September 2012.*

*Next the line reaches Afflington Bridge where it passes under the A351 main road to Swanage. Corfe Castle ruins are still clearly visible in the far distance as the ex-LSWR M7 Class 0-4-4 Tank **No.53** approaches the bridge on its way towards Swanage. 28 July 2012.*

The ex-GWR 0-6-2T **No.6695** pulls into Harmon's Cross Station after leaving Corfe Castle. This totally new double track station was built since the railway has been in heritage hands. Situated roughly halfway between Corfe Castle and Swanage it now provides a very suitable location for trains to pass. 28 July 2012.

*Viewing the overall scene as BR Standard Class 4 **No.80104** awaits clearance to proceed at Harmon's Cross, it is hard to believe that this station did not exist at all during the golden age of steam days and only opened to traffic in 1989. 9 September 2012.*

*As we continue our journey along the line we catch a glimpse of **No.34028 Eddystone** once more, but this time it has just left Harmon's Cross Station and is running tender first towards Swanage. 24 April 2011.*

Left: *BR Standard Class 2 2-6-0* **No.78019** *waits at Harmon's Cross for rebuilt West Country Class 4-6-2* **Eddystone No.34028** *to arrive from Swanage and transfer passengers. 9 September 2012.*

*Ex-BR Standard 2-6-4 Tank locomotive **No.80104** passes the Swanage Station signal box having just coasted under Northbrook Road Bridge which frames the entrance to the station complex. 30 July 2011.*

Left: *Travelling through the outskirts of Swanage before it reaches the town centre terminus. Ex-GWR 0-6-2 Tank **No.6695** heads a mixed freight towards Swanage Station. 9 September 2012.*

The proximity of the town centre can clearly be seen as we pull into the Swanage Station rail terminus, The adjacent station siding usually has something of interest on display and this time it is one of the railway's diesel multiple units. 25 May 2012.

Right: *At our journey's end, BR Standard Tank **No.80104** comes to a halt at Swanage Railway's southernmost terminus and head-quarters, Swanage Station. The 'run around' loop in the track can clearly be seen as can the railway's crane and a brake van which are parked on display in the station siding. 7 April 2012.*

*On the return journey from Swanage Station we are treated to a very rare scene, a double-headed train pulled by two Southern Region West Country Class Pacific locomotives. Un-rebuilt **No.34070 Manston** leads rebuilt **Eddystone No.34028** which is masquerading as an unkempt **Bodmin No.34016** – sans nameplate as it would have appeared just before being withdrawn from service in 1964 – out from platform 2 during Swanage Railway's Grand Steam Gala and Vintage Transport Rally. 8 September 2013.*

WEST SOMERSET RAILWAY

History of the West Somerset Railway

The current line is 22 miles in length and like so many others has a complex history. The line was opened by the original West Somerset Railway in 1862 between Taunton and Watchet and then extended from Watchet to Minehead in 1874 by the Minehead Railway. Although the Minehead Railway was absorbed into the GWR during 1897, the West Somerset Railway remained a separate entity right up until the 1921 Railways Act forced an amalgamation. The entire line from Taunton to Minehead continued to boom and expand through to the middle of the twentieth century when, like so many others, it went into steady decline.

During the boom period, stations were extended for longer trains and many passing loops were built where the line was still single track. However, decline became fairly rapid after the railways were nationalised in 1948. Washford signal box closed in 1952, Minehead engine shed in 1956 and Norton Fitzwarren Station shut in 1961. All goods traffic was withdrawn from the line by 1964 and the Minehead turntable plus much track was removed in 1967. The entire line was finally closed during 1971 followed by the lifting of much more of the track.

Later in 1971, Minehead Railway Preservation Society organised a meeting and the West Somerset Railway Company was formed to acquire the line and initially operate a commuter service from Minehead to Taunton. Although this plan failed, in 1973 Somerset County Council bought the line from BR to prevent the potentially lucrative Minehead Station site falling into private hands and the line was then leased back to the West Somerset Railway Company. The task of reinstating a railway was massive as there were no locomotive facilities left at Minehead, nearly all the rails had been lifted and all the signalling equipment had gone. Yet in 1976 the heritage line managed to open the Minehead to Blue Anchor section and shortly after the line was connected through to Williton. Trains returned to Stogumber by 1978 and finally reached Bishops Lydeard in 1979. In 1987 WSR built a totally new Halt at Doniford.

Two miles further up the line from Bishops Lydeard, the West Somerset Railway still has a mainline rail connection at Norton Fitzwarren where another brand new halt and a turning triangle (officially opened in 2012) for locomotives has been built.

*We start our photographic journey along the West Somerset Railway at the new Norton Turning Triangle, where we see Sir Nigel Gresley's magnificent LNER A4 Pacific **No.4464 Bittern** traversing the tracks, so that it can run chimney first on its return journey from Bishops Lydeard to Minehead. 21 June 2012.*

Although the railway is operated by the West Somerset Railway Company, it is supported by a number of voluntary and charitable organisations:

The *West Somerset Railway Association* based at Bishops Lydeard, is the supporting charitable body of the railway. The Association recruits and looks after the volunteers and also some of the locomotives.

West Somerset Steam Railway Trust acts as a repository for the safe keeping of items of railway interest which may be donated, loaned or bequeathed. The Trust is concerned with the historical and educational aspects of railway preservation in West Somerset and assists with various restoration projects such as steam locomotives and historic railway items for use on the WSR.

West Somerset Restoration based at Williton Station provides a heavy engineering facility complementing those at Minehead. It is managed and funded by the WSRA with the primary objective to support and maintain the WSRA locomotives.

The *Diesel and Electric Preservation Group* was formed to promote interest in the modern railway scene. After providing excellent diesel locomotive restoration work to the WSR, the group became formally responsible for Williton goods shed in 1986 and focused all resources there in 1991.

Somerset and Dorset Railway Trust, although dedicated to all matters relating to another– the Somerset & Dorset Joint Railway (SDJR). It restored track and facilities on the West Somerset Railway at Washford where it has a museum and restoration workshop. It also owns the SDJR No.88 engine which is extensively used by the WSR.

Website links:

- Further information on West Somerset Railway Plc (WSR) can be obtained from their website – *www.west-somersetrailway.co.uk*
- Further information about the West Somerset Railway Association (WSRA) can be obtained from their website – *www.wsra.org.uk*
- Further information about the West Somerset Steam Railway Trust (WSSRT) can be obtained from their website – *www.wssrt.co.uk*
- Further information about West Somerset Restoration can be obtained from their website – *www.wsrestoration.co.uk*
- Further information about the Diesel and Electric Preservation Group (DEPG) can be obtained from their website – *www.depg.org*
- Further information about the Somerset and Dorset Railway Trust (SDRT) can be obtained from their website – *www.sdrt.org.uk*

Track layout and Stations

At approximately 22 miles in length, the West Somerset Railway is one of the longest heritage railways in the UK. Upon leaving Bishops Lydeard the track heads northward through open farmland and hamlets along the foot of the Quantock Hills while climbing steeply to the highest point on the line at Crowcombe Heathfield. The subsequent long descent winds through woods, cuttings and embankments to Stogumber where it clings to the hillside for a short while before opening out. The line then crosses the A358 into woods at Castle Hill before arriving at Williton. A flat meandering course now takes the train to Doniford Halt from which it bursts out onto the edge of the Bristol Channel before heading west towards Watchet through cliffside cuttings.

Leaving the harbour at Watchet, the line runs back inland through the town on a south-west bearing, climbing steeply once more to the village and station at Washford. The route exits Washford via a short cutting then drops through trees turning northwest heading back to the Bristol Channel across open plains into the coastal village and station at Blue Anchor. From Blue Anchor an open run west crosses Ker Moor and hugs the shoreline for a few miles before departing slightly inland across flat open plains to Dunster Station. From here a short straight track leads to the West Somerset Railway's terminus in the seaside town of Minehead.

Bishops Lydeard: Lying 4 miles from Taunton, this station is the current southern terminus of the West Somerset Railway. It has two platforms with double track between and an adjacent secure locomotive compound. On platform 1, the original buildings from 1862 include the old station master's house and the goods shed which now houses a railway museum and model railway exhibition. The Whistle Stop Café on platform 2 serves a variety of hot and cold snacks. The station has a booking office and souvenir shop which also sells railway books, videos and models. There is free parking, toilets, baby change facilities and the disabled are well catered for. It is also home to the WSRA.

Crowcombe Heathfield: Having no nearby villages, this quintessential GWR country station is run by volunteers and frequently used for period films. When closed in 1971 the station still had neither electricity or gas and was lit by oil lamps! On the up platform the station has a booking office and waiting room where snacks and drinks are served. A small waiting room and signal box sit on the down platform. Other facilities include toilets and limited parking.

Stogumber: An unusual little station in that it has been built on a hillside ledge necessitating the main buildings to be housed on the opposite side of the track to its single platform – which has to be accessed via a crossing. Largely demolished by BR after closure, restoration of outbuildings and compounds are still actively being undertaken by FoSS (Friends of Stogumber Station). Facilities include a lineside memorial garden/picnic area, toilets, waiting room and cream tea refreshments.

*At Bishops Lydeard Station ex-GWR 2884 Class 2-8-0 **No.3850** awaits on platform 1 for SDJR **No.88** to exit from platform 2, both heading for Minehead on the first day of the West Somerset Railway Winter Steam Gala. 28 December 2011.*

*Heading north after leaving Bishops Lydeard the line runs elevated past the village of Combe Florey. Here we see ex-GWR 2884 Class 2-8-0 **No.3850** pulling a rake of Chocolate and Cream-liveried carriages across Combe Florey Bridge, climbing up towards the highest point on the line at Crowcombe Heathfield. 28 December 2011.*

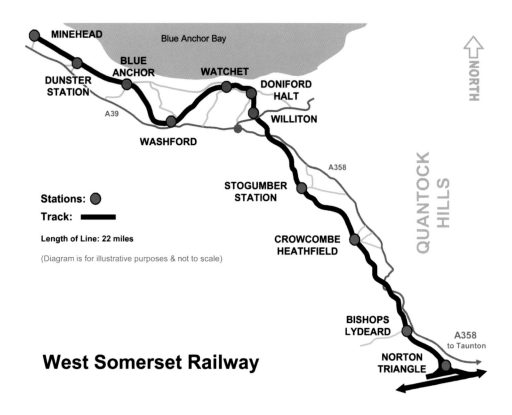

West Somerset Railway

Length of Line: 22 miles

(Diagram is for illustrative purposes & not to scale)

Stations: ●

Track: ▬

Blue Anchor Bay

MINEHEAD

BLUE ANCHOR

WATCHET

DONIFORD HALT

DUNSTER STATION

WILLITON

A39

WASHFORD

NORTH

STOGUMBER STATION

A358

QUANTOCK HILLS

CROWCOMBE HEATHFIELD

BISHOPS LYDEARD

A358 to Taunton

NORTON TRIANGLE

Williton: Built on the edge of the town and re-opened in 1976, the two platforms on this double track station are far apart due to the original line being built for Brunel's 7ft Broad Gauge. The signal box harks back to the station's Bristol and Exeter Railway days but the footbridge was re-instated in 2012. The goods shed is home for the DEPG and has a visitor centre open at weekends. Another ex-GWR works shed (which was acquired from Swindon) is the restoration base of the WSRA and the WSSRT. Locos awaiting restoration can often be seen adjacent to platform 1. Facilities include parking, a booking office, waiting room, toilets (not disabled) and a small gift shop.

Doniford Halt: This request stop recreates a typical GWR wayside halt and was newly built in the 1980s to serve a nearby holiday centre. There are no facilities bar a corrugated iron GWR 'pagoda' shelter which was rescued from Cove.

Watchet: The single platform and line stands in the heart of this ancient seaport town next to the harbour. The station building is strangely at right angles to the track which is due to Watchet being the original terminus of the West Somerset

*Crowcombe Heathfield is the first station on from Bishops Lydeard. As we enter from the south, we meet WSR's own 2-6-0 Mogul **No.9351*** returning from Minehead during the Jubilee celebration week. 4 June 2012.*

* Still surrounded in controversy by purists, this hybrid locomotive is the result of a radical rebuild. West Somerset Railway created this very practical Small Mogul to an originally proposed GWR design, from a scrapped Large Prairie Tank No.5193. Following GWR practice for the first of a new class it has been given the number 9351.

Railway. The station has a refurbished footbridge which was erected in 2012, a booking office, waiting room and a small shop selling souvenirs, biscuits and drinks. Toilets with disabled facilities and council parking are also available.

Washford: Now home to the Somerset and Dorset Railway Trust who have set up a museum and restoration workshop on the site of the old goods shed and yard. This single platform village centre station has toilets and offers only light refreshments. Built slightly later and differing in style from earlier buildings on the line, the station is also painted in Southern Region colours as opposed to GWR. Street parking is limited.

Blue Anchor: Originally opened as Bradley Gate, this seaside station grew along with the popularity of Blue Anchor as a resort. The single beach-facing platform was extended to two with double track in 1904. The long platforms house a restored booking office and waiting room serving light refreshments, toilets, a small museum and a signal box which still controls the level crossing gates via a traditional capstan wheel. Camping carriages situated on the former goods yard provide accommodation for WSR volunteers. There is ample sea front parking.

Dunster: A five minute walk from the beach and twenty from Dunster village and castle, this delightful little single platform station was copied by Hornby for their railway models. Opposite is the goods shed – now home to WSR's Permanent Way department, who maintain the bridges, stations and buildings etc – which is reputed to be haunted! There is parking, a booking office and toilets, but no disabled facilities.

Minehead: Now the WSR's head office, this town centre station grew from a tiny terminus in 1874 to quarter mile long platforms by 1933, but that was before the decline! Now not only beautifully restored, in 2008 a whole new visitor experience was created with the installation of a locomotive turntable with public viewing area, plus the Turntable Café. A large signal box busily controls train movements over the road crossing and the former goods shed has been extended to become a steam locomotive restoration workshop. Comprehensive facilities include: café, booking office, and toilets with disabled and baby changing. The station shops stock gifts, books, DVDs, models and clothing. Adjacent parking is council run.

Norton Fitzwarren: Two miles towards Taunton from Bishops Lydeard, a new halt was built at Norton Fitzwarren along with a turning triangle for steam locomotives. First proposed by the WSRA in 2004, the four coach platform was first used for the 2009 Steam Fayre held on that site. 2012 saw the triangle in use on gala days, thus for the first time ever on a heritage railway (and in conjunction with the Minehead turntable at the other end of the line) allowing all steam engines to be run 'chimney first'. There is currently no external public access to this halt, but there are lots of future plans for this site.

*Our second stop along the line is Stogumber Station. It is unusual in that the platform is set on the opposite side of the line to the main station building and picnic area. The ex-SDJR 2-8-0 **No.88** has just arrived from Crowcombe Heathfield and readies to continue its journey toward Minehead on a December afternoon. 29 December 2011.*

West Somerset Railway typical 'standard' daily timetable example

Below is an example of a typical WSR Green Timetable (6 trains in each direction). Although the times are typical, they should not be taken literally as times may be adjusted from season to season as needs change. However it does give an idea of the frequency of trains and travel times between stations on a 'normal' day.

GREEN TIMETABLE (Mixed traffic example Steam & Diesel timetable)							
		Steam	Diesel	Steam	Steam	Diesel	Steam
BISHOPS LYDEARD	Depart	**10.25**	**11.40**	**12.35**	**14.20**	**15.10**	**16.10**
CROWCOMBE HEATHFIELD	Depart	10.40	11.51	12.51	14.36	15.27	16.25
STOGUMBER	Depart	10.48	11.59	12.59	14.44	15.35	16.34
WILLITON	Depart	11.00	12.11	13.12	14.58	15.55	16.52
Doniford Halt *(Request)*	Depart	11.04	12.14	13.15	15.01	15.58	16.55
WATCHET	Depart	11.11	12.20	13.21	15.08	16.05	17.00
WASHFORD	Depart	11.19	12.28	13.29	15.17	16.12	17.08
BLUE ANCHOR	Depart	11.26	12.44	13.38	15.24	16.23	17.15
DUNSTER	Depart	11.33	12.51	13.45	15.31	16.30	17.22
MINEHEAD	Arrive	**11.40**	**12.58**	**13.52**	**15.38**	**16.37**	**17.29**
		Steam	Steam	Diesel	Steam	Steam	Diesel
MINEHEAD	Depart	**10.15**	**12.30**	**13.20**	**14.15**	**16.05**	**17.35**
DUNSTER	Depart	10.22	12.37	13.27	14.22	16.13	17.42
BLUE ANCHOR	Depart	10.30	12.45	13.40	14.30	16.22	17.50
WASHFORD	Depart	10.38	12.53	13.48	14.38	16.31	17.58
WATCHET	Depart	10.48	13.02	13.56	14.47	16.41	18.06
Doniford Halt *(Request)*	Depart	10.51	13.05	13.59	14.50	16.45	18.09
WILLITON	Depart	11.00	13.12	14.05	15.01	16.50	18.14
STOGUMBER	Depart	11.13	13.25	14.14	15.14	17.03	18.23
CROWCOMBE HEATHFIELD	Depart	11.23	13.34	14.38	15.25	17.12	18.31
BISHOPS LYDEARD	Arrive	**11.33**	**13.44**	**14.48**	**15.35**	**17.22**	**18.41**

NOTE: Doniford Halt is a Request Stop only.

A Red Timetable (4 steam trains in each direction) runs just as frequently and also on winter days. During peak season seven trains normally operate, five steam and two diesel. Very busy timetables are published for the special galas, late night specials and other frequent events. For these, times are always posted separately and are available from the WSR website – *www.west-somerset-railway.co.uk*

LOCOMOTIVES ON THE WEST SOMERSET RAILWAY   Circa 2012/2013

The list below is only intended as a guide to stock recently associated with the line.

STEAM LOCOMOTIVES

Number/Description		Condition/Info
34046 *Braunton*	SR West Country Class 4-6-2	Serviceable
9351	GWR/WSR Mogul Class 2-6-0	Serviceable

7828 *Norton Manor*	BR Class 4-6-0	Serviceable
88	SDJR 7F Class 2-8-0	Serviceable
7821 *Ditcheat Manor*	BR Class 4-6-0	Awaiting overhaul
3850	GWR 2884 Class 2-8-0	Serviceable
4160	GWR/BR Large Prairie 2-6-2T	Serviceable
5553	GWR Small Prairie 2-6-2T	Withdrawn 2012 for overhaul
6960 *Raveningham Hall*	GWR Class 4-6-0	Serviceable @ WSR 2012
Kilmersdon	Peckett 0-4-0 Saddle Tank	SDRT Demonstration shunter
4561	GWR Small Prairie 2-6-2T	Stripped for overhaul

DIESEL LOCOMOTIVES

Number/Description		Condition/Info
D1010 *Western Campaigner*	Class 52 Western C-C	DEPG owned
D832 *Onslaught*	Class 42 Warship B-B	DEPG owned
D1661 *North Star*	Class 47 Brush Co-Co	DEPG owned
D6566 *Crompton*	Class 33 Bo-Bo	DEPG owned
D6575	Class 33 Bo-Bo	
D7017	Class 35 Hymek B-B	DEPG owned
D9526 *Teddy Bear*	Class 14	DEPG owned
D2133	Class 03 0-6-0	
D2271	Class 04	
D3462/08377	Class 08 0-6-0	
DH16	Rolls Royce Sentinel 0-4-0	DEPG depot shunter
No1 & No2	Andrew Barclay 0-4-0DH	Depot shunter
No24	Ruston & Hornsby 0-4-0DM	SDRT Washford shunter

DIESEL MULTIPLE UNITS

Number/Description		Condition/Info
51880	DMU Class 115	Serviceable

*Continuing on our journey north, the WSR Mogul **No.9351** double-heads a morning train with the ex BR Standard Class 7 4-6-2 Pacific locomotive **Brittania No.70000**. They are seen here descending the steep bank at Bicknoller through open pasture between Stogumber and Williton. 18 March 2012.*

*Coming back south from Williton engines have their work cut out as they start the very long steep uphill climb towards Stogumber and on through to the line's summit at Crowcombe Heathfield. Here ex-GWR 4-6-0 **Norton Manor No.7828** is captured working hard in mid summer less than a mile from Williton Station at Castle Hill. 4 June 2012.*

Carriages and Wagons

Most West Somerset Railway trains are formed from British Rail Mark 1 TSO coaches painted in Chocolate and Cream livery based on the GWR colour scheme but with their own WSR crests.

There are numerous types of goods and freight wagons located along the railway in various sidings and at stations. Some are fully operational but others are for display, awaiting restoration, or for heritage demonstration train purposes only.

*The ex-SDJR 2-8-0 **No.88** heads south from Williton Station towards Bishops Lydeard. 5 October 2012.*

*Exiting Williton Station past a locomotive repair depot and continuing north towards Minehead is **Tornado**, the steam engine which surprised the world. After nineteen years of incredibly hard work by the A1 Steam Locomotive Trust to build and operate a brand new Peppercorn class A1 Pacific locomotive, the result was **Tornado** an LNER 4-6-2 **No.60163** which first powered under its own steam in 2008. It was the first brand new main line steam locomotive to be built in the UK for over fifty years. 28 June 2011.*

The next stop en route is the request halt at Doniford, which comprises a short curved platform with a tiny GWR metal pagoda waiting room.

*West Somerset Railway's Mogul **No.9351** pauses for passengers to alight and due to the curve of the platform the engine driver has to hang out of the cab to check for the all clear to proceed. From here the line now turns west hugging the coast to Watchet. 28 December 2011.*

*Heading west away from Watchet **Raveningham Hall No.6960** approaches the old Mineral Line Bridge. From here the line loops inland to Washford before returning to the coast once again at Blue Anchor. 28 December 2011.*

Left: *On a late summer afternoon Mogul **No.9351** approaches Watchet Station from Doniford Halt. 28 June 2011.*

From Watchet and still heading west, ex-GWR Modified Hall Class 4-6-0 locomotive **Raveningham Hall No.6960**, *double-heading with GWR King Class 4-6-0* **King Edward 1 No.6024**, *arrive at Washford – a village centre station. 24 March 2012.*

*Washford Station on the WSR is currently run by the Somerset and Dorset Railway Trust and these two fine ex -SDJR locomotives **No.88** a 2-8-0 and diminutive 0-4-0 **Kilmersdon** are demonstrating shunting during the WSR Cambrian Railways Gala. 5 October 2013.*

*Under an overcast autumn sky, ex-LMS Stanier Class 5 (AKA Black 5) **No.45379** double-heads an LMS Ivatt Class 4 **No.43106** across Ker Moor heading towards Blue Anchor on an up-bound passenger train from Minehead. 5 October 2012.*

Left: *Arriving from Minehead and heading towards Bishops Lydeard, SDJR 2-8-0 **No.88** enters Blue Anchor Station across the B3191 road crossing on the west side of the coastal station. 7 October 2012.*

*We are now at the penultimate stop on our journey along the line and find the 'auto-fitted' ex-GWR 0-6-0 Pannier Tank **No.6430** along with its accompanying Autocoach briefly pausing for passengers at Dunster Station whilst operating a special gala shuttle service between here and Minehead Station. 24 March 2011.*

Right: *Ex-GWR 4-6-0 **Raveningham Hall No.6960** exits Minehead bound for Bishops Lydeard. 22 March 2012.*

With our journey along the line completed, another is seen here in preparation. Visiting WSR for the 2011 Spring Steam Gala, ex-Southern Railway King Arthur class 4-6-0 **Sir Lamiel No.30777** is turned on the new Minehead Station turntable ready for its return run to Bishops Lydeard. 19 March 2011.

Left: Our journey along the line ends on the coast at Minehead Station which is WSR's main terminus. Here we are treated to a rare sight indeed, a matched pair of ex-GWR 4-6-0 Hall Class locomotives making ready to depart from Minehead. **Kinlet Hall No.4936**, double-heads an up-bound train to Bishops Lydeard with **Raveningham Hall No.6960**. 5 October 2012.

APPENDIX

GLOSSARY OF TERMS

Double Heading: Two locomotives coupled together to pull a train.

Double Track: A railway line with two tracks, one for each direction.

Down: See 'Up'.

Halt: A station where trains stop by request.

Island Platform: A platform which has track either side.

Mixed Train: A train comprised of both passengers and goods.

Passing Loop: A single line branching to two lines running parallel for a short run to either allow, two trains to pass each other, or a locomotive to 'run around', i.e., go to the other end of a rake of carriages.

Terminus: A station at the end of the running line (plural - termini).

Token: An object used for safety in single line working. To proceed on a single track line, an engine driver must be in possession of the token. Having reached a position of safety, the token is then passed on to the next train needing to run in the opposite direction. Hence only one train can be on that single line at any one time.

Top and Tail: A train with a locomotive at either end.

Up: The term 'up' refers to a direction on the line pointing towards London and conversely, 'down' refers to a direction on the line pointing away from London. This stems from Britain's rail network, which certainly in its early days spread out like a web from London, to various rail termini around the country. i.e. An 'up-train', or an 'up-bound' train, is a train travelling along the line in a direction, in such a manner that if it continued it would eventually reach London and the 'up-platform' is the platform you would use to get on that train. A 'down-train' from a 'down-platform' will take passengers in a direction away from London.

KEY TO LOCOMOTIVE AND ROLLING STOCK FORMER REGIONS AND OWNERSHIP

GWR:	Great Western Railway	**LNER:**	London & North Eastern Railway
LSWR:	London & South Western Railway	**SR:**	Southern Railway
LMS:	London Midland & Scottish Railway	**BR:**	British Railways

LOCOMOTIVE CLASSIFICATIONS: WHEEL ARRANGEMENTS AND POWER

Due to varying line requirements it became necessary to classify locomotives to help identify which were most suited for various locations and tasks.

In the UK wheel arrangements use a notation such as 2-6-0, this notation counts the number of *leading wheels*, then the number of *driving wheels*, and finally the number of *trailing wheels*, the numbers being separated by dashes. A few of these wheel arrangements also have names in common use.

Notation	Profile	Name
0-4-4T		
4-4-0		
0-6-0T		
4-4-2		Atlantic
2-6-0		Mogul
2-6-2T		Prairie
4-6-0		
4-6-2		Pacific
2-8-0		

A 'T' suffix after the wheel arrangement notation indicates that the engine is a Tank engine, i.e., the engine carries its own coal and water on board. At times this is often conjoined with another letter to denote the type of tank locomotive and more specifically, where it carries its on-board water supply. T is a Side Tank, PT is for a Pannier Tank, ST a Saddle Tank and WT is for a Well Tank locomotive. No suffix indicates a Tender Locomotive, i.e., the engine tows its coal and water in a wheeled trailer directly behind, known as a Tender.

During the British Railways period a system of classification to indicate Power and Usage (developed from an earlier LMS system) was also used, where 'Power' was rated from 1 to 9 (9 being the most powerful) and 'Usage' by the letters 'P' for Passenger, 'F' for Freight and where an engine was equally suited to both uses 'MT' for Mixed Traffic.

For example: A Class 4MT locomotive has a power rating of 4, for both freight and passenger work.

When used these British Railways classifications were written directly above the engine number on the side of the cab.

THE AUTHOR'S PHOTO GALLERY

Adrian Harris is a passionate steam railway enthusiast with a love of photography. Many of the photographs which accompany this book can be viewed alongside other favourites from the author's own railway photo collection at:

www.majestyofsteam.co.uk

The night train awaits at Buckfastleigh.